WALK SUTHERLAND

50 Graded Walks
in the
Northern Highlands of Scotland

Sutherland Tourist Board commissioned Tom Strang, Proprietor Assynt Guided Holidays, Knockan, Assynt, Sutherland, to write this book, the companion volume to his very successful "Hillwalker's Guide to Sutherland".

Acknowledgements

I would like to thank Jonathan Shepherd, Caithness & Sutherland Walks Officer, Donald McNeill, Stephen Fraser and Pete Williams of Forest Enterprise, and Valerie Wilson, Alex Scott, Chris Wright and Fraser Symmonds of Scottish Natural Heritage for their help and advice in planning walks for this book.

I would also like to thank my old friend Bill Wallace for writing the Foreword, and Norman MacCaig for his permission to use extracts from his marvellous poem "A man in Assynt". Also Norman MacAskill, Lochinver, and John Gibson, Unapool for their helpfull comments on specific points in the text, and Mr and Mrs Christopher MacKay, Armadale, who were an invaluable source of information on their former family roots in Poulouriscaig.

Garry Allighan, Alba Cartographics, Stoer, has produced the excellent sketch maps, and Trish Mathews, "Hands On", Dornoch for her illustrations.

Finally, I would like to thank David Richardson, Chief Executive of Sutherland Tourist Board, both for his contributions and for his invaluable role as editor.

ISBN 0 9522654 0 0

While every effort has been made to ensure that the information contained in this publication is accurate, Sutherland Tourist Board accepts no responsibility for errors or omissions, for subsequent alterations to routes, or legal responsibility for any accidents or damages, however caused.

Front Cover Photograph — David Richardson.

Back Cover Photograph — Tom Strang.

First Published by Sutherland Tourist Board Ltd. 1995.
Reprinted by The Highlands of Scotland Tourist Board 1997.

Printed by The Northern Times Ltd., Main Street, Golspie, Sutherland KW10 6RA

Extracts from

A man in Assynt

by Norman MacCaig

Who owns this landscape?
Has owning anything to do with love?
For it and I have a love-affair, so nearly human
we even have quarrels. —
When I intrude too confidently
it rebuffs me with a wind like a hand
or puts in my way
a quaking bog or a loch
where no loch should be. Or I turn stonily
away, refusing to notice
the rouged rocks, the mascara
under a dripping ledge, even
the tossed, the stony limbs waiting.

I can't pretend
it gets sick for me in my absence,
though I get
sick for it. Yet I love it
with a special gratitude, since
it sends me no letters, is never
jealous and, expecting nothing from me, gets
nothing but
cigarette packets and footprints.

Who possesses this landscape? —
The man who bought it or
I who am possessed by it?
False questions, for
this landscape is
masterless
and intractable in any terms
that are human.
It is docile only to the weather
and its indefatigable lieutenants —
wind, water and frost.

Sutherland — A Land of Contrasts

Foreword by Bill Wallace, Secretary, John Muir Trust;
Past President, Scottish Mountaineering Club

Many friends had praised Sutherland as a county of contrasts and fond memories, and had urged me to see the place for myself. It was thus with considerable anticipation that my wife and I drove north to spend our honeymoon in the village of Stoer. In those days — and it is not so many years ago — all the roads were nine feet wide with passing places and so progress was leisurely. With no pressures of time we were able to relax and delight in unusual and varied scenery and climate.

It was some years after this that I met Tom Strang, author of the last two district guides to the area published by the Scottish Mountaineering Club, and also of the companion volume to this one, *A Hillwalker's Guide to Sutherland*. His unrivalled knowledge of this part of the country makes him admirably qualified to write a walking guide to Sutherland for all tastes and abilities.

Tom lives at Knockan, some 20 miles north of Ullapool, where he has built the excellently appointed Birchbank Holiday Lodge from which he acts as a guide to walkers, hill climbers and anglers. The view from the picture window in the Lodge of the hills of the Inverpolly Reserve must rank with the best anywhere.

Inevitably, after the first visit, I have returned many times, visiting the vast, largely uninhabited, moorlands in the east as well as the uniquely isolated hills of the west, and the scenic, cliff-girt coasts. I have a vivid memory of camping *en famille* behind the dunes at Sandwood on an evening in early summer watching the sun, a glowing red orb, set in a cloudless sky over the sea. On another occasion, when we walked to Cape Wrath, the weather was quite the opposite, with heavy, wind-driven squalls of rain coming in off the sea. The rivers were running high and were difficult to cross, but the coastal scenery was magnificent, especially at the Cape, with its colonies of cliff-nesting seabirds. And talking of seabirds, no-one should miss a visit to Handa Island, where the horizontal sandstone ledges of the Great Stack are so crowded with guillemots and other birds that there scarcely seems room for the birds flying in to jostle their way on to the ledges.

I remember, too, when Sutherland was enjoying a prolonged heat wave — yes, it does happen. We had borrowed canoes from friends in Ullapool and launched them into Loch Veyatie. Following a leisurely paddle along to the far end of the loch and a perspiring climb up the west nose of Suilven, we eventually reached the summit at 8 o'clock at night. My most vivid memory, however, is of paddling back along the loch in the semi-darkness, trying unsuccessfully to close with the red-throated divers.

But it is not always like that. One Easter, (I was staying at Birchbank), when the weather had been wet for several days, it seemed a good opportunity to see Britain's highest waterfall, the Eas a'Chuil Aluinn, at its most wild and spectacular. We were very wet but not disappointed.

To appreciate Sutherland fully, many visits are necessary — if possible at all times of year. Nevertheless, even the first-time visitor will surely agree that the contrasts of climate and scenery make the country worth visiting again and again. Happy walking.

SUTHERLAND

David Richardson, The Highlands of Scotland Tourist Board

Geography

Sutherland is the most northerly district of the Scottish Highlands. With an area of 2,200 square miles (5,700 square kilometres) it is also the largest, and its population of 13,100 makes it one of the least densely populated areas in Europe — under 6 people per square mile.

Sutherland has three coasts — a wild and rugged west coast, indented with numerous sea lochs and bays, separated by rocky headlands; a wild and rugged north coast with fewer sea lochs and more cliffs; and a softer, gentler east coast consisting of long stretches of golden sand. All coastlines offer excellent walking.

Within this landmass lie several distinct regions.

To the west, a broad band of rugged and rocky hills runs north/south down the coast, rising out of a plateau of hard gneiss rock. This is an area of fascinating geology, and many of the isolated hills are famous for their unusual and dramatic shapes — hills like Suilven and Arkle. Innumerable lochs and lochans stipple the ground, and are drained by short, swift rivers, many containing salmon. The people live in small fishing and crofting communities, generally on the coast.

Moving eastwards, the hills subside into rolling, heathery moorland drained by long rivers flowing north and east. Modern forestry plantations hug the lower hillsides, while blanket peat bog is to be found over much of the centre and north — the famous "Flow Country". This country is remote, wild, and largely empty of people, most people living on the north coasts, and in the larger straths (valleys). It is wonderful country — but great care must be taken when walking through it, both for your own preservation, and for the preservation of wildlife, especially in the breeding season.

The moorland continues east until it meets a narrow band of hills overlooking an even narrower fertile coastal plain running down the coast. The tree-lined Dornoch Firth lies on the Ross & Cromarty border to the south, while the hilly, cliff-fringed Ord of Caithness is on the Caithness border to the north. The east coast contains the best agricultural land in Sutherland and it is also the most populated part, but even here, communities are small, close-knit and traditional.

10,000 YEARS OF HISTORY IN SUTHERLAND

David Richardson, The Highlands of Scotland Tourist Board

The First People — Man has lived in Sutherland since the end of the last Ice Age, some 10,000 years ago. For the first 4,000 years, small groups roamed the land hunting herd animals like reindeer on the tundra, then, as the climate warmed and vegetation spread, they hunted woodland animals like red deer, and gathered fruit, roots, nuts and shellfish — their 6,000 year old stone tools have been found on the East Coast.

The Neolithic — The first farmers arrived between 5,000 and 6,000 years ago and started to clear the forests, grow crops and keep livestock. Their presence is indicated by the great chambered cairns (burial mounds) and stone circles that are frequently found overlooking the straths and glens.

The Bronze Age — began at around 2,000 B.C. — the population was increasing rapidly and small farms sprang up in every fertile strath and glen. Evidence for this can be seen in the numerous round house foundations (hut circles) which dot the landscape (many are of Bronze Age origin), in the small fields surrounded by banks, and in the scattering of clearance cairns (stones moved off the arable land and dumped in piles). Bronze Age burial cairns are also to be seen.

Towards the end of the Bronze Age the climate began to deteriorate, becoming colder and wetter. The land was also being over-cultivated, and this, together with the climatic change, led to the spread of peat which began to engulf the settlements and fields, leading to their abandonment. Population pressure increased on the better land in the valley bottoms.

The Iron Age — began in about 800BC and effectively lasted at least until 1,000AD. The deteriorating climate saw cereal crops being replaced by vegetables, and a major shift towards cattle as the main food source. Cattle are valuable and are easily moved, and this, together with increased population pressure, meant that there was a sudden, widespread appearance of defensive structures at this time — defended homesteads, hill forts, duns, and brochs. This is thought to be the birth of chieftain society, tribal warfare and cattle raids - a way of life that was to last until only 250 years ago!
The builders of these structures were later known as Picts — they had no writing but they were accomplished artists, producing magnificent symbol stones such as those at the Strathnaver Museum, Bettyhill and the Dunrobin Castle Museum, Golspie.

Viking Invasions — Pictish dominance was soon to end. Scots arrived in Strathclyde from Ireland in around 500AD and gradually expanded their territory by winning land from, and intermarrying with, the Picts. Meanwhile, Vikings were beginning to raid the northern coasts. From 800 onwards, these Norsemen began settling in Orkney and they soon crossed the Pentland Firth and colonised Caithness and then much of Sutherland. Sutherland was their "Southern Land", its boundary being the Dornoch Firth. Cape Wrath, on the north-west tip of Scotland, means "turning point" and was where their galleys turned south down the western seaboard.

Clans and Battles — The Norman Scottish noble families were next to make their presence felt, the lucky few being granted lands in Sutherland. The next five hundred years saw much feuding between these families or clans, each striving to gain more land or power. This was a time when a Chief's wealth was measured by the number of fighting men he could command. Great clans like Sutherland, Sinclair, MacKay, Murray and MacLeod all tried to gain the upper hand, and castles such as Caisteal Bharraich (Castle Varrich), Ardvreck, Skelbo and, greatest of all, Dunrobin all bear witness to these turbulent times. Clearances, Crofting and Fishing — The Clan system gradually started to break down and this was accelerated after the 1745 Rising when many chiefs had their estates forfeited, and others headed for the easy life in Edinburgh and London, leaving their people to eke out a living on their meagre land — the ordinary people lived very hard lives, frequently having to contend with famines and disease. Chiefs no longer required fighting men, but they did require income to support southern lifestyles. The demand for wool was growing (for soldiers in the Napoleonic Wars) and the Highlands were seen as ideal for sheep — if only the people would get out of the way.

At first the people went voluntarily to settle the Colonies or to look for work in the industrial towns of the south. However, this emigration was thought too slow, and early in the last century there began the Sutherland Clearances, when families were thrown out of their homes which were then burnt down. Families were left destitute, some to find their way to the coast to start fishing, some to go south, and others overseas. Many of the original "pre-clearance" settlements are to be seen in Strathnaver and Kildonan. Croick church is well worth visiting, while the displays in the Strathnaver Museum and at Timespan, Helmsdale are superb.

While the Clearances were a terrible blight on the people and have left many deep scars, money was invested in the economy of the area — model villages like Helmsdale were established, and fishing and the improved agriculture was encouraged. In the middle of the last century crofting began, with many safeguards to protect the small farmer or crofter. Crofting continues to the present day, largely as a part time occupation. While crofting was becoming established on the land, herring fishing was booming at sea and harbours like Helmsdale and Lochinver became important as bases for large fishing fleets.

Today — the economy is still largely based on primary industries like farming, forestry, fishing and fish farming. Tourism is another vital industry — the emphasis very much being on ecologically sound "sustainable tourism".
Sutherland has always suffered from poor agricultural land, lack of raw materials, extremely low population density, remoteness from industrial centres and markets — the list is long. However, Sutherland also has many strengths, and there are currently a number of public agencies seeking new solutions to old problems, solutions that are in keeping with the hopes and aspirations of the people and with the splendour of the environment.
It is to be hoped that disparate ventures like Hunters new woollen mill in Brora, the Carnegie Club at Skibo Castle, and the Assynt Crofters Trust on the West Coast will only be the first of many steps towards a prosperous future.

WILDLIFE IN SUTHERLAND

Sutherland's unique geology combined with the effects of the weather and the influence of Man has created a fascinating and diverse range of wildlife habitats. Mountain, moorland, bogland, woodland, farmland, sea cliffs, sandy beaches — it is no surprise that Sutherland has one of the greatest ranges of flora and fauna in Britain.

This is just a taste of what lies in store!

Plants

Sutherland is particularly suited to arctic and alpine plants. Mountain plants such as *moss campion, mountain avens* and *purple saxifrage* occur almost down to sea level. The coastline supports a wide range of plants, including rarities like the *oysterplant,* while some clifftops boast *spring squill* and *primula scotica* — the *Scottish primrose,* which can be found only in Sutherland, Caithness and Orkney.

Inland, the great expanse of the "Flow Country" contains a wide range of exotic plants, including *bog asphodel, bogbean, sundews* and the insect-eating *butterwort.*

Birds

Birds are abundant in Sutherland at all times of the year. The mountains are home to *golden eagles, ptarmigan* and *ravens,* while the moorlands contain *peregrine falcons, hen harriers, red grouse* and *meadow pipits.* From April to July the blanket bogs of the "Flow Country" are home to breeding *greenshank, dunlin, golden plover, common scoter,* and both *red-* and *black-throated divers.*

The seacliffs of the north and west coasts have vast colonies of *guillemots* and *kittiwakes,* and *puffins* may also be seen, while the Dornoch Firth and Loch Fleet shelter thousands of wildfowl over the winter months — rafts of up to 3,000 *eider ducks*, 3,000 *velvet scoters*, 4,000 *long-tailed ducks* and 8,000 *widgeon. Osprey* numbers are rising, the birds being best seen fishing in the sea off south-east Sutherland and in inland lochs and rivers.

Animals

Red deer are to be found throughout the whole area, while *roe* and *sika deer, wild cats, pine martens, red squirrels, foxes* and *badgers* live in the woodlands. *Blue hare* live on moorland and mountainsides, while *otters* may be seen on river banks or around the coasts.

Brown trout are found in most lochs, *sea trout* in a few, and *arctic charr* in fewer still. One of the most spectacular sights is the *salmon* leaping up waterfalls as they return upstream to spawn.

Offshore, there are two types of *seal* — *grey* and *common* — and *porpoises, dolphins* and *whales* may sometimes be seen.

Note: many of the animals and plants listed here are extremely rare and are protected by law. Please treat all wildlife with respect and keep away from young animals and from nesting birds — it is illegal to photograph some nesting birds. Dogs must also be kept under control at **all** times.

FINDING OUT MORE

Museums and Visitor Centres

This book can only give you a taste of the character of the land you will pass through — its geology and geography, fauna and flora, archaeology and history — and the character and culture of its people.

Much more information is available from Sutherland's museums and visitor centres — this list is complete at time of writing.

1.   Bettyhill, Strathnaver Museum

Located in the former Bettyhill Church, the museum features the archaeology and history of the North Coast and the life and times of its people — especially Clan MacKay. Open Easter — October. Entry Fee.

2.   Dornoch, Old Post Office Visitor Centre

Located within the Tourist Information Centre — snapshots of South East Sutherland — history, geography, places to go and things to see and do. Old Post Office counter and photographic collection. Open all year. Free.

3.   Durness Visitor Centre

Located within the Tourist Information Centre — informative panels on the North West tip of Scotland — its geology, geography, archaeology and history. Also Countryside Ranger base — guided walks and talks — and geological display outside. Open Easter — October. Free.

4.   Forsinard, Flow Country Visitor Centre

Located in the old station building — information on what the Flow Country is, where it is and why it is special — flora and fauna. Open Easter — October. Free.

5.   Golspie, Dunrobin Castle, Museum & Gardens

The seat of the Earls and Dukes of Sutherland, dates to 13th century. Magnificent interiors — furniture, paintings and silver. Museum includes fine collections of local geology, archaeology and natural history. Open Easter, and May — October. Entry Fee.

6.   Golspie, Orcadian Stone Company

Includes collection of rocks and fossils from the Northern Highlands. Open all year. Entry Fee.

7.   Helmsdale, Timespan Visitor Centre

Thousands of years of Highland history and culture — from earliest time to the present day — presented in dramatic displays and tableau. Audio visual presentation. Also Highland medicinal and culinary herb garden. Open Easter — October. Entry Fee.

8.   Knockan, Knockan Cliff Visitor Centre

This small centre features the geology and natural history of the Inverpolly area. Geology trail and nature trail along limestone cliffs (Walk 50). Seasonal. Free. No dogs.

9.   Lairg, Ferrycroft Countryside Centre

The past, present and future of woodlands in the Northern Highlands — their influence on Man, and Man's influence on them. Audio-visual displays, touch table. Tourist Information Centre. Picnic tables, children's play area, archaeological trail and forest walk (Walk 22). Open Easter — October. Free.

10.   Lochinver, Assynt Visitor Centre
Displays on the landscape and scenery, wildlife and people of this wild West Coast parish. Crofting, fishing and wildlife explained. Gaelic pronunciation booth, local archive, Countryside Ranger base, Tourist Information Centre. Geological display outside. Open Easter — October. Free.

Several new visitor centres/interpretive centres are currently being developed — ask at Tourist Information Centres for details of new openings.

Books and Guides
Many books have been written about Sutherland and the Northern Highlands, and many more include extensive coverage of the area.

Listed below are some of the more prominent which may be available from Tourist Information Centres and local book shops.

General and Area Guides

Empty Lands — A Guide to N W Scotland	T Atkinson	Luath Press
Land of Rocks & Lochs — Assynt & Lochinver	ed N Kerr	Glatea (UK) Ltd
What to See Around Bettyhill	KJ O'Reilly	
What to See Around the Kyle of Tongue	KJ O'Reilly	
Tales of the North Coast	A Temperley	Luath Press

Geology & Scenery

Highland Geology Trail	JL Roberts	Strathtongue Press
Assynt Geological Motor Trail	DR Shelley	Sutherland Tourist Board

Birds

Sutherland Birds	ed S Angus	The Northern Times Ltd

Archaeology & History

Exploring Scotland's Heritage — Highlands	J Close-Brooks	HMSO
Scotland BC	A Ritchie	HMSO
Invaders of Scotland	Ritchie & Breeze	HMSO
Highland Clearances	J Prebble	Puffin
Highland Clearance Trail	R Gibson	Highland Heritage Educational Trust
The Ord, Lairg — a Journey Back in Time	C Wickham-Jones	The Highland Council

Walking & Climbing

Hillwalker's Guide to Sutherland	T Strang	Sutherland Tourist Board
Guide to North West Scotland	Bennet & Strang	Scottish Mountaineering Club
Exploring the Far North West Scotland	R Gilbert	Cordee
The Corbetts and Other Scottish Hills	Bennet and others	Scottish Mountaineering Club
Safety on the Mountains		British Mountaineering Club
Forests of Caithness & Sutherland — Walks		Forestry Commission

ACCESS

Each year sees more and more people making use of the countryside for recreation, enjoying a wide variety of pastimes, interests and active sports. However, many visitors with fairly modest aspirations as explorers are deterred from venturing far from the roadside because they are unsure of what they are allowed to do or where they are allowed to walk.

Scotland has a long tradition of freedom of access to the countryside within reasonable limits — a fortunate situation which can only be maintained given responsible behaviour on the part of all users. Access for recreation does not always go hand in hand with traditional country practices such as agriculture, forestry and estate management, but given a reasonable attitude on both sides, there need be no conflict.

It should be remembered that unrestricted access is only permitted on proven rights of way in Scotland — elsewhere, access is by permission of farmer, landowner or manager. So when walking is over private land used for any other activity, a common sense approach makes life easier for everyone.

Various national bodies closely connected with recreational use of the countryside — Forest Enterprise, Scottish Natural Heritage, Mountaineering Council for Scotland, Scottish Landowners Association, and others — have published policies on access with accompanying lists of simple guidelines — common sense and consideration is the theme throughout.

Respect private property at all times and keep to paths when going through farmland and estates. Popular paths are susceptible to erosion through constant use, and despite repair work, they are always vulnerable. Everyone who walks established paths can help maintain their usefulness. Keep on the path and don't cut corners, especially on zig-zag descents. Don't walk abreast on paths — this is the quickest way of creating unsightly, broad, "motorways" across the countryside. Where sections of the path have been repaired, use them — respect diversions around badly worn areas. Don't add to existing marker cairns or erect new ones which could be misleading.

Use gates and stiles where possible instead of climbing over fences and walls — and remember — always close gates after you.

Guard against fire, especially in forest parks, and protect trees, plants and wildlife. Many of our designated Nature Reserves are particularly vulnerable, especially those in coastal areas. Don't leave any litter, it is unsightly and can be dangerous to animals — picnic by all means, but what you bring out full you can take back home empty — *take nothing but photographs* — *leave nothing but footprints.*

Many people make their living from apparently wild stretches of countryside, and some times of the year are more important to them than others:-

Lambing — the season varies according to the area, in Sutherland it is generally between late March and the end of May. Keep dogs under control at all times and especially during the lambing season. Sheep are killed each year by family pets, and they can easily miscarry their lambs if stressed. Sheep farmers are entitled to shoot dogs found worrying sheep — never put the life of your dog at risk!

Red Deer Stalking — The open season for culling red deer stags is from 1st July — 20th October, and for hinds from 21st October — 15th February. However, the most critical period is generally from mid-August to mid-October. Ask locally if in doubt — most reasonable estates will indicate an alternative walks if stalking has been planned over your proposed route. Remember — your presence can not only ruin a days stalking — it also puts your own life in danger.

Grouse Shooting — The season is from 12th August — 10th December, with most shoots during the earlier months. Nesting birds on moorland are vulnerable, however, so walkers should take care at nesting times.

Man is not the only inhabitant of the countryside — please take the greatest care not to disturb wildlife, especially during the breeding season.

In Forest Parks access is generally unrestricted — visitors are welcome and well-catered for by Forest Enterprise. In most cases walking routes have been facilitated by the erection of gates, styles and by prominent yellow way-marker discs. However, it is your duty to:-

Guard against fire at all times and avoid damage to trees, buildings, fences, hedges, walls and signs within the forest area.

Respect the work going on in the forest and keep away from any operations for safety reasons. Don't obstruct gates and remember that vehicles are not allowed within the forests except by prior arrangement.

Obtain permits for horse riding, fishing and other special activities, if in doubt, ask at the local forest district office. The carrying of firearms or other weapons is strictly forbidden.

Respect the peace and quiet of the forest and avoid disturbing others.

Sutherland is special, and if it is to remain so we must all respect it and do nothing that might bring it harm —

> "Let no one say,
> And say it to my shame
> That all was beauty there
> Until I came"
>
> (Anon)

Walking in Sutherland

Safety —
This book describes routes in detail and includes basic maps to illustrate the text. Many walks are straightforward and simple, requiring moderate fitness and the minimum of experience or equipment. However, others are harder and take you into wilderness areas where weather conditions can change very rapidly.

To help you select the right walks for you, a simple system of grading has been used:

Grade A   Easy routes suitable for all age groups — generally level walking, mostly on paths, tracks, or easy hillsides.

Grade B   Intermediate routes of varying length — a mixture of paths and open ground giving uncomplicated wayfinding. Generally suitable for family walks allowing ample time.

Grade C   More demanding routes — either because of length or type of terrain covered. For fitter experienced walkers with basic navigational skills.

Equipment
The recommended footwear is indicated at the start of each walk — though you should pay attention to current weather conditions. When in doubt, wear comfortable walking boots.

You should always carry a map with you — Ordnance Survey 1:50,000 Landrangers are generally best — and for longer walks you should also carry — **and know how to use** — a compass. Landranger map numbers are given for each walk, as are grid references for key points along the route.

You should also carry water-/wind-proof outer clothing, hat and gloves, and also hot drinks, sandwiches and high energy food such as mars bars where appropriate.

Transport
While most walks in this book are circular, some require two cars, and many are a considerable distance from the nearest village or from bus or train routes. A private car is therefore essential for most walks, and where a walk does start on a bus or train route, the service may be very infrequent. You should seek advice from Tourist Information Centres when planning a walking holiday without a car.

Accommodation
A wide range of comfortable accommodation to suite all tastes and pockets is to be found in almost every village and township (hamlet) around the area. Detailed lists of hotels, guest houses, bed & breakfasts, self catering cottages and campsites can be obtained from local Tourist Information Centres, or from Scottish Tourist Board — Tel 0131 332 2433.

Tourist Information Centres

Bettyhill	(Easter - September)	01641 521342
Dornoch	(All Year)	01862 810400
Durness	(Easter - October)	01971 511259
Helmsdale	(Easter - September)	01431 821640
Lairg	(Easter - October)	01549 402160
Lochinver	(Easter - October)	01571 844330

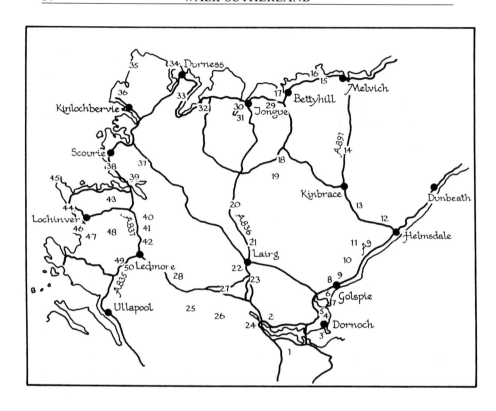

RED DEER STAG

CONTENTS

		Grade	Page
1.	Struie Hill, Dornoch Firth	B	17
2.	Loch Migdale and the Fairy Glen	A	18
3.	Dornoch Links	A	20
4.	Dornoch to Embo	A	21
5.	Skelbo Forest Walk & Sculpture Trail, Dornoch	A	23
6.	Balblair Wood and Loch Fleet	A	24
7.	Littleferry and Ferry Links, Golspie	A	25
8.	Beinne a' Bhragaidh (Ben Bhraggie) and the Monument, Golspie	B	26
9.	Big Burn Waterfall, Golspie	A	29
10.	Duchary Fort & Carroll Rock — Strath Brora	B/C	30
11.	The Hills of Glen Loth	C	32
12.	Kilphedir Broch — Strath of Kildonan	B	34
13.	Sutherland Gold — Suisgill Burn & Cnoc na Beiste — Strath of Kildonan	B/C	36
14.	The Borg to Dyke — Strath Halladale	B	38
15.	Armadale Bay and Gorge	A	39
16.	Poulouriscaig — The Deserted Village	A	41
17.	Invernaver & Torrisdale Bay	B	42
18.	Rosal Clearance Village, Strathnaver	A	44
19.	Clach an Righ (The King's Stone) and Truderscaig, Rosal, Strathnaver	C	46
20.	Crask Inn to Bealach Easach and Ben Klibreck	B/C	48
21.	Dalchork Wood, Lairg	A	50
22.	Ord Hill Archaeology Trail & Shin Dam Forest Walk, Lairg	A	52
23.	Shin Falls Forest Walk	A	54
24.	Carbisdale Castle Forest Walk & Battlefield	A/B	56

		Grade	Page
25.	Croick Church to Oykel Bridge	C	57
26.	Croick Church to Alladale and Craigs	C	60
27.	Ravens Rock Forest Walk, Rosehall	A	61
28.	Craggie to Loch Ailsh, Strath Oykel	B/C	62
29.	Borgie Forest Walk	C	64
30.	Caisteal Bharraich (Castle Varrich), Kyle of Tongue	B	65
31.	Lochan Hakel & Bonnie Prince Charlie's Gold, Kyle of Tongue	B	67
32.	Arnaboll, Loch Hope	B	68
33.	Loch Eriboll Wheelhouse	B/C	70
34.	Balnakiel & Faraid Head, Durness	A/B	72
35.	Cape Wrath to Sandwood Bay and Blairmore	C	74
36.	Blairmore to Sandwood Bay	B/C	77
37.	Around Ben Stack, Achfary	B/C	78
38.	Loch a'Mhuillin, Duartbeag	A	80
39.	Kylestrome to Loch Glendhu	B/C	81
40.	Eas a'Chual Aluinn (waterfall) and the Marble Road from Inchnadamph	C	83
41.	The Caves of the Traligill Glen, Inchnadamph	A	86
42.	Allt nan Uamh Bone Caves, Inchnadamph	A/B	88
43.	Gleann Leireag from Loch Assynt	B	90
44.	Clachtoll from Achmelvich, Assynt	B/C	92
45.	Stoer Head and the Old Man, Assynt	A	94
46.	Culag Wood, Lochinver	A	96
47.	Inverkirkaig Falls & Fionn Loch, Assynt	B	98
48.	Glen Canisp to Elphin, Assynt	C	100
49.	Uamh an Tartair, Knockan, Assynt	B	102
50.	Knockan Cliff & Nature Trail	B	103

1 Struie Hill, Dornoch Firth

Grade:	**B**
Distance:	**7 kilometres.**
Footwear:	**Walking boots**
Terrain:	**Suitable for fit families.**
Time:	**2½ hours.**
Map:	**OS Landranger 21.**

The Dornoch Firth was once a formidable barrier separating Sutherland from Easter Ross. Struie Hill is best seen from the Dornoch Firth Bridge, but its broad-topped ridge, which undulates north-eastwards along the south shore of the Dornoch Firth for almost 3 kms, dominates the lands around the Firth.

The ascent is straightforward, making a fine introduction to a walking tour of Sutherland.

The starting point is the Cadha Mor pass on the A836 road that links the Cromarty and Dornoch Firths. This road meanders across the rounded hills of the Easter Ross peninsula — a scenic route reminiscent of a more leisurely age of travel. This was a cattle drovers' route — the traditional gateway between the remote straths and mountains of Sutherland and the markets of the south. "Cadha Mor" is the Gaelic for the "great entry point".

Stop at the viewpoint to savour the magnificent panorama across the Dornoch Firth to the Kyle of Sutherland and beyond.

The Route

1. Retrace the road southwards from the viewpoint for 800 metres to reach a stone bridge and parking area for one or two cars (GR651850). The walk starts

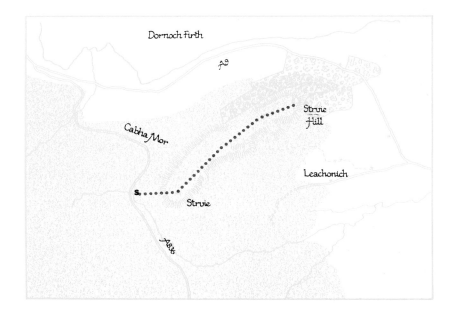

some 30 metres north where a well-worn track leaves the east side of the road opposite an overgrown quarry hole.

2. Follow the path up heathery slopes to pass a conifer plantation on its north edge. The path swings away from the trees before climbing steeply onto the summit of the ridge (371m), skirting the edge of a prominent rocky outcrop as it does so.

3. From there, the radio mast, which stands at the north-east end of the ridge (approx 2.5 kms away), is almost always in view, and wayfinding is easy. The surface is generally firm and covered with short heather, though there are one or two softer, deeper patches. The higher points along the way are cairned. A track is joined for the final 800 metres and this can be seen winding up onto the ridge from the farmlands below.

The views across the Dornoch Firth from the summit are wonderful. To the west lie Ardgay, Bonar Bridge, and the Kyle of Sutherland, gateway to the wilds of the West and North. Cattle swam the Kyle at Am Bhannath — the crossing place — near Bonar Bridge in the old days. Directly in front, on an impressive tree-lined headland, is Dun Creich — the most northerly Iron Age vitrified fort in Britain. Across the bay stands a ruined cotton mill at Spinningdale — destroyed by fire in 1808. To the east, the new Dornoch Firth Bridge spans another old crossing point — the Meikle Ferry was the main crossing point for traffic heading north. The Royal Burgh of Dornoch guards the sandy point at the north-east corner of the Inner Firth, while the Royal Burgh of Tain lies on the south shore. On the coastline beyond Dornoch, the controversial statue of the Duke of Sutherland is seen on Beinn a' Bhragaidh, above the family seat at Dunrobin Castle, Golspie.

4. Return by the same route or make a circle by using the track descending eastwards from the mast.

2 Loch Migdale And The Fairy Glen

Grade:	**A**
Distance:	**10 kilometres**
Footwear:	**Walking boots or wellingtons**
Terrain:	**A splendid family walk, full of interest for all ages — some wet patches!**
Time:	**3½ hours**
Map:	**OS Landranger 21**

Loch Migdale is one of the largest of the inland trout lochs in the south-east corner of Sutherland. It lies in a granite basin just north of the main A9 road, hidden among a landscape of varied woods (mainly oak and Scots pine), and rolling croftland. This is an area rich in history; outstanding finds of Early Bronze Age metal work, dating from before 1500 BC, were found at the west end of Loch Migdale early this century. Numerous remains of early settlements can be traced, and Neolithic chambered cairns — circa 3000BC — lie on south facing hillsides. There are records from the 17th Century of an artificial island at the west end of the loch on which stood a crannog (lake-dwelling). This area, the "Fairy Glen", was one of Andrew Carnegie's favourite spots when he lived at Skibo Castle near Dornoch at the start of this century. Fish farming (salmon) has been a recent development there.

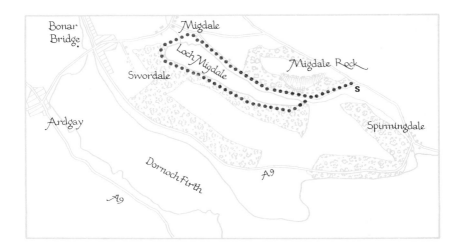

Leave the A9 road at Spinningdale, 8 kms east of Bonar Bridge. A single track road leads north-west from the petrol station past crofts and through woodland towards the "Fairy Glen" and Migdale. After 2 kms, look for a track on the south side of the road which leads into the woods on that side of the glen (Woodland Trust Signpost); parking is possible with care at the roadside (GR664908).

The Route

1. Follow the track through the mixed woodland for 1.5 kms to reach the east end of Loch Migdale — the rounded grey granite hump of Migdale Rock towers above the tree line — a pleasant route, rich in bird life. The track keeps to the north shore of the loch for 3 kms (level but slightly wet in place), eventually breaking clear of the trees to cross open croft land. Leave the track where it rises towards the road to Migdale crossroad.

2. The section of the walk around the north-west corner of the loch involves crossing two small streams (around GR632917) — not usually difficult depending on weather. A sheep path is eventually joined at the extreme west corner, which leads back through the woods along the south shore of the loch for just over 3 kms. Follow a track around the end of the loch to rejoin the route followed on the outward walk.

BURIAL CAIRN

3 Dornoch Links

Grade:	**A**
Distance:	**Flexible — 4 kilometres plus**
Footwear:	**Good walking shoes**
Terrain:	**Beach/dunes and hard tracks — excellent family walking for all ages and interests.**
Time:	**Flexible according to route**
Map:	**OS Landranger 21**

One of the finest attractions of the ancient Royal Burgh of Dornoch is the links and beach area around which it has developed and which forms the foundation of its world-famous golf course. The sandy beaches, which stretch almost unbroken for 9 kms from Dornoch Point to Loch Fleet, and for many more kilometres to

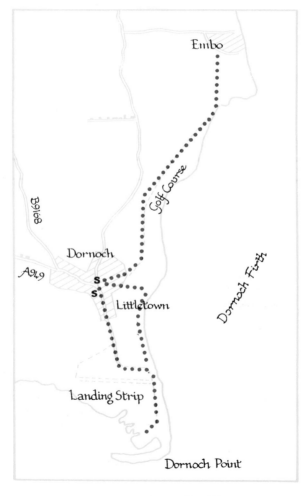

the north of that, offer countless combinations of bracing walks for all weather conditions.

Enter Dornoch and park in the Square outside the Tourist Information Centre & Old Post Office Visitor Centre. Dornoch is a Royal Burgh with a long and interesting history — the Cathedral dates back more than 750 years. Visit the Tourist Information Centre & Old Post Office Visitor Centre to find out more about this area.

The Route

1. Leave the Square at its east end and turn right down Church Street, past the Dornoch Inn. Continue on this road to the small cottages of Littletown — the last garden on the left contains a stone marked "1722". This was the site and date of the last witch-burning in Scotland — the sad story is well told in the Timespan Heritage Centre in Helmsdale. (Note — the garden is private). Just northeast of this is the "Witches Pool", where captured German guns were dumped in protest by ex-servicemen after being brought back as trophies from the First World War.

2. Follow the tarred road southwards for 1 km across the smaller of Dornoch's two golf courses, to reach the small aircraft landing strip. A path (no cars) leads east onto the dunes and beach from where it is a further kilometre to Dornoch Point. As you reach the Point look seawards to the east to where the waters are in a state of perpetual motion — this is the Gizzen Briggs, where the "little people" work endlessly at low tide to build a bridge of sand across the Firth, only to have it washed away by every incoming tide! Look out for common seals. The flat land on the south side of the Firth is an airforce target range — you might see jets practising.

3. Return back along the beach to the carpark beside the inshore rescue boat station, and follow the road past the Golf Club back to the Square. (If there has been recent rain you will have to paddle across the burn half way along the beach).

---

4 Dornoch To Embo

Grade:	**A**
Distance:	**10 kilmometres**
Footwear:	**Walking shoes**
Terrain:	**Good track and beach — easy for all ages and abilities**
Time:	**2½ - 3 hours**
Map:	**OS Landganger 21**

Although only about 5 kms apart, Dornoch and Embo are very different. While Dornoch began as a religous centre and has a long and noted history, Embo's origins lie in the Highland Clearances, the village having been founded in around 1820 for people cleared from the inland straths and glens. It was originally a fishing village, and the traditional cottages all run in rows down to the sea.

Although a fairly modern village, Embo has been the site of much past activity — it contains a Neolithic chambered cairn (in use for over 1,500 years into the Bronze Age), and it was also the site of a battle in 1245 when a band of marauding Norsemen was driven off by local forces, the Viking chief being killed by a horse's leg wielded by local knight Sir Richard de Moravia!

Much of this walk is along a disused railway track — Dornoch was linked to the main North Line in 1902 in recognition of the town's importance as a resort for the rich and famous. The line closed in 1960 — though the town still attracts the rich and famous!

The Route

1. Leave the Tourist Information Centre and follow the road to Embo from the east end of the Square. Stop at the interpretive panel on the north side of the High Street bridge — it marks the site of the old monastery well, and the board includes a map of mediaeval Dornoch. Continue north along the pavement to reach the entrance to the Industrial Estate. This is on the site of the Dornoch Railway Station. On the opposite side of the Embo road you will see a signposted path leading up into the Scots pines of Station Hill. Follow this path which runs parallel to the road. At the minor road, cross straight over and enter the wooden gate on the other side — do not walk up the private drives to the houses. The path runs between two houses and then enters the wood once more — follow it round the hill, keeping to the right (upper) path until you reach another sign pointing you down the hill to the left. Follow this to the edge of the wood (GR802903).

2. Leave the wood and follow the path to the right (east) over the rough grassland to a style. You will see the Earl's Cross stone to your left — it marks the boundary between the lands of the Earls of Sutherland and the Church. Stand on the style and look around you. To the east lies Royal Dornoch Golf Course and the sea — the mouth of the Dornoch Firth — with Tarbet Ness Lighthouse at the tip of Easter Ross some 14 kms away. To the south lies Dornoch, Easter Ross, and in the far distance, the Cairngorm Mountains. To the west you will see a patch-work of small farms and crofts, and to the north . . .your route.

3. Turn left (north) and follow the path along the top of the bank beside the golf course — please do nothing to disturb the golfers.

4. After about 1 km you will meet a gate beside the golf course at the top of a hill. The railway line bears slightly left, keeping on top of the bank, and follows the fence to Embo — you should do the same.

As you approach Embo you will see that it consists of a cluster of cottages and that there is a large caravan park beside it. The caravan park — Grannie's Heilan' Hame, incorporates the original "Highland home" immortalised in the Scots song. Beyond Embo you will see the hills of East Sutherland leading north to the Ord of Caithness.

5. From Embo you can return by the same route, or you can walk through the caravan park to the harbour and follow the beach back to Dornoch.

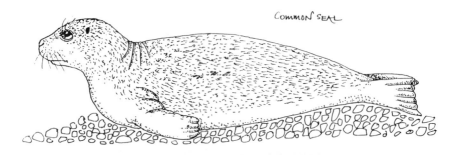

COMMON SEAL

5   Skelbo Wood Forest Walk & Sculpture Trail

Grade: **A**
Distance: **3 kilometres**
Footwear: **Good walking shoes**
Terrain: **An easy circular family walk through beautiful woodland.**
Time: **1½ hours**
Map: **OS Landranger 21**

This is one of a series of forest walks created by Forest Enterprise as part of their policy of improving access to the countryside.

Turn east off the A9 road at the telephone box 1.25 kms north of the Trentham Hotel (GR779941), and follow the single track road (signposted "Skelbo") for a short distance to a Forest Enterprise signpost. Enter the woods and park in the designated area.

The Route

1. A signposted path leads east for a short distance through mature conifers to join a more prominent track. Follow this north across a track junction to pass (and inspect) the remains of a Broch standing on the east side, continue to an open clearing in the trees with a viewpoint seat.

2. Follow the path down into the gorge of the Skelbo Burn and head west. The burn banks have been cleared of conifers to allow the mature beech and other deciduous woodland to thrive. A brick building contains a hydropneumatic ram which once pumped water to surrounding highlying farms.

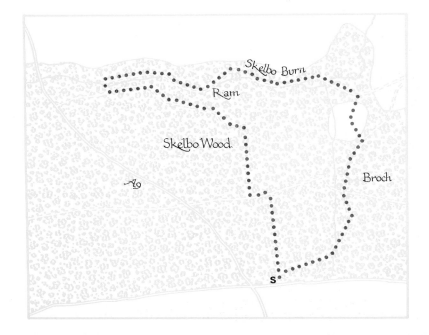

3. Re-cross the burn by a footbridge and follow it eastwards to reach a seat, from which point the path ascends steadily back to the start.

An interesting feature of this walk are the wood carvings by local Forest Enterprise Forest Officer, Peter Bowsher. The carvings are based on drawings of woodland birds and animals by local Dornoch Primary School children, and all are carved entirely by chain saw.

6   Balblair Wood And Loch Fleet

Grade:	**A**
Distance:	**8.5 kilometres**
Footwear:	**Walking boots or wellingtons**
Terrain:	**Flat woodland track and shoreline — wet in places. Wayfinding is comparatively easy — a good family walk with lots of wildlife. If walking the shoreline remember tide times and the danger of the strong currents within the basin**
Time:	**2½ hours**
Map:	**OS Landranger 21**

The broad tidal basin of Loch Fleet indents the coast line midway between Dornoch and Golspie. In 1816, the famous builder of Highland roads, bridges and Parliamentary churches, Thomas Telford, constructed an embankment or "Mound" across its narrow neck as part of an ambitious bridge building programme — it still carries the main A9 trunk road north. To the west of the causeway, unsuccessful efforts were made at land reclamation, and today the Mound Alderwoods are a National Nature Reserve. To the east, the main basin of Loch Fleet is renowned for its populations of waders and wildfowl, easily seen from both shores. The whole area is within a Scottish Wildlife Trust Reserve.

Leave the A9 road from the signposted junction at the children's playground at the west end of Golspie (signposted Littleferry and Golf Course), and follow the minor road south across Golspie Links and through a wood for 3 kms until the estuary is reached on the right hand (west) side of the road. Park in the picnic area (GR811972), which contains a large panel identifying the birds of the mudflats.

The walk can be shortened by parking at the woodland gate on the right-hand (west) side of the road (GR815977), taking care not to block the road or gate.

The Route

1. Leave the car and follow the burn on the west side of the road north to reach a track. Turn right over the wooden bridge and follow the track into the woods for about 1 km until an obvious crossroad is reached. There are now three alternatives — 2c is recommended.

2a The north branch reaches a pedestrian gate at the edge of the Reserve after 300 metres, from where it joins up with a rough motor track which leads out for another kilometre to exit on the A9 trunk road 3 kms west of Golspie. Motor access on this track is restricted and any walkers should beware of trains — the route crosses the main line just before it reaches Kirkton Farm.

2b The south branch from the crossroad emerges from the trees after a short distance onto the open shoreline of Balblair Bay.

2c It is easiest to continue west along the main track through the woods until the estuary is reached. Follow the shoreline back (east) to Balblair House (boarded up), and then take the track back to the crossroad, turning right to return to the start.

Alternatively, you can stay on the coast until the burn is met and follow it up to the bridge that you crossed at the start.

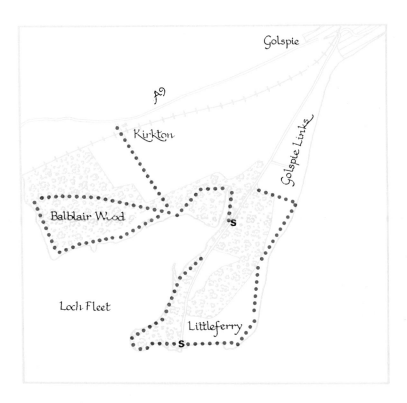

7 Littleferry And Ferry Links

Grade:	**A**
Distance:	**8 kilometres**
Footwear:	**Walking shoes or wellingtons**
Terrain:	**Level and easy, though stony shoreline at (3.). Interesting and enjoyable.**
Time:	**2½ hours**
Map:	**OS Landranger 21**

Leave the A9 at Golspie on the same road as for Walk 6 and follow it south to its end. Just before reaching the houses you will see a carpark on the left hand side of the road (park in the second carpark).

Littleferry is a cluster of cottages on the north shore of the narrow mouth of

Loch Fleet. As the name suggests, it was once the main crossing point for traffic heading north or south over the Fleet. It was also a 19th Century trading station (for coal, meal, salt and lime for agricultural improvements), and all the buildings had a particular function. An interprative panel in the carpark tells the story and identifies the ferryman's house, the pilot's house, the customs and mussel inspector's house, as well as the girnal (for grain), the ice house (for fish), and the stores for sails, rope, and other provisions.

The surrounding links is covered in plants and flowers, and Man's presence here over thousands of years is demonstrated by the occasional discovery of stone tools.

The Route

1. Leave Littleferry and follow one of the paths eastwards along the outflow of Loch Fleet to its mouth.

2. Head north along the beach (or stick to the links) for just over 2 kms, to reach the go-kart track which lies at the north end of the conifer plantation. Follow this west for 400 metres to reach the road. You can either follow this road for 3 kms back to the car, or. . . .

3. Walk south along the road for 1.5 kms, and then leave it and follow the shoreline south-west around the edge of the little point for around 2 kms to its western tip. Look out for seals. From there, turn east along the edge of the shore, to pick up the track at the Girnal (house) and follow it back to the carpark.

8 | Beinne A' Bhragaidh (Ben Bhraggie) And The Monument

Grade:	**B**
Distance:	**7 kilometres**
Footwear:	**Walking boots**
Terrain:	**Very steep path, eroded in places, open moorland on summit. No technical difficulty but requires effort — a steady pace on the way up helps the enjoyment of the view at the summit.**
Time:	**2½ hours**
Map:	**OS Landranger 17**

Like many well-known hills in Sutherland, Beinne a' Bhraggie's isolated position 2 kms north-west of Golspie greatly enhances its fairly modest height. In addition, its 394 metre summit carries a 30 metre high statue & plinth commemorating the 1st Duke of Sutherland. Commissioned after his death in 1834, the statue was originally destined for the top of Ben Klibreck, a Munro summit in the centre of his 1,000,000 acre estates. However, the plan proved too ambitious, and the statue now guards the south side of Dunrobin Glen, looking seawards across the Moray Firth, where it can be seen from miles around. The Highland Clearances of the early 19th Century were a time of misery and hardship in the Highlands, and the name of the 1st Duke of Sutherland will be linked forever to this period. At the time of writing a debate is rageing throughout the Highlands about whether the statue should remain on the hill.

On a clear day, the views from the summit are breath-taking — well worth the effort.

Leave the A9 road on Fountain Road in the centre of Golspie and park in the carpark.

The Route

1. Continue up the road, past the fountain, under the railway bridge, past Rhives House and farm to a further junction.

2. Take the left branch up the rough track past a water tank and continue up the hill, climbing gradually at first through the trees. There are frequent new path markers along the way.

3. Pass under power cables to reach a prominent cross track. Beyond this, the wood is more dense and the path becomes significantly steeper and more eroded towards its final section at the top of the treeline. Cross a stile onto open heather and follow the well-trodden way upwards — there is a short, steep section before the base of the statue. A breathtaking view awaits!

4. Continue north-west from the statue and follow the wide vehicle track which winds across the open summit plateau before descending, regaining the woods 2 kms from the statue.

5. After a further 800 metres you reach a crossroad. Turn right (south), and follow the prominent track for 1 km to reach the point where you crossed it on your outward walk. Descend the path back to the start.

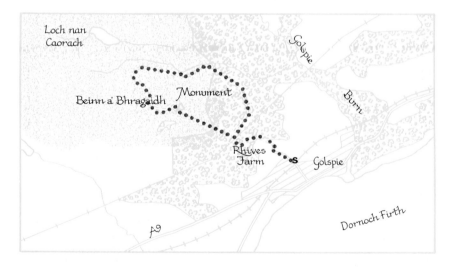

STATUE OF FIRST DUKE OF SUTHERLAND
ON BEN BHRAGGIE

9 | Big Burn Waterfall, Golspie

Grade:	**A**
Distance:	**3 kilometres**
Footwear:	**Stout shoes, boots or wellingtons**
Terrain:	**Mostly on made paths and forest tracks, but some wet patches. An easy family walk, full of nature and open to variations of route and distance.**
Time:	**1 hour plus.**
Map:	**OS Landranger 17**

Golspie's Big Burn follows an 8 kms course from its source in Loch Horn through Dunrobin Glen to the sea. The final stretch through mature mixed woodland, contains one of the finest woodland walks in the country. The spectacular 16m waterfall halfway down the wooded gorge is bridged both above and below for closer viewing, and the rich variety of woodland plants and birds are seen at their best by the early season visitor.

Leave the A9 road 1 km north of Golspie, turning left (west) under a railway bridge (signposted "Backies"). Continue for just over 1 km to reach the Big Burn

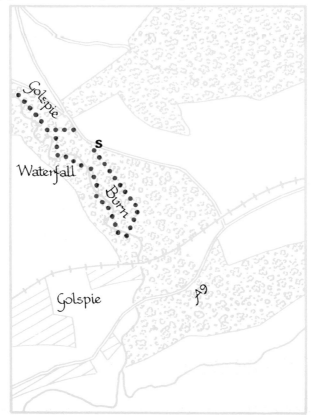

Car Park and Picnic Place on the thickly wooded north bank of the stream. The new interpretive board there details routes which can be followed and special viewpoints along the way. The entire layout of the paths and bridges has been recently upgraded by local volunteers with commercial sponsorship, the project winning the Scottish round of the Shell Better Britain campaign for 1994 and being Highly Commended for the UK as a whole. Plans are in hand to rebuild most of the bridges over the next few years, and this will affect the geography of the walks.

The Route

1. For a circular route from the carpark, follow the path westwards taking an almost level line towards the waterfall. The path forks, both branches eventually leading down to a natural viewing platform which gives a superb view of the falls.

2a From the platform, one branch of the path continues west towards Backies, forking left to cross the top of the falls by a new footbridge, and then winding down onto the south side of the gorge

2b The other branch turns back downhill into the gorge, crossing onto the south side by a footbridge at the base of the falls from where it links with the first branch. A detour to the foot of the falls leads onto a cantilever viewing platform over the plunge pool.

3. From the bridge where the paths join, the route crosses the still rocky course of the burn three more times then stays on the north side. The floor of the gorge widens and the waters of the burn no longer tumble down over shelves and ledges.

4. Leave the now gentle burn bed by a path which climbs steeply onto the rim of the valley, and then turn west through the conifers to return to the carpark.

10   Duchary Hill Fort & Carrol Rock — Strath Brora

Grade:	**B/C**
Distance:	**16 kilometres**
Footwear:	**Walking boots**
Terrain:	**Tracks, open moorland and heather. A scenic walk for the family with plenty of heritage interest.**
Time:	**4 hours (less 1 hour if Carrol Rock is omitted)**
Map:	**OS Landranger 17**

Strath Brora is one of the most populated of the great eastern straths which open out from the central Sutherland hills. The River Brora, a salmon water of note, follows its bed throughout. Loch Brora, a picturesque loch some 6 kms long, fills the strath 6 kms inland from the old town of Brora. Evidence of early inhabitants abound in the shape of the old settlements, brochs and defensive forts which are found scattered about the sheltered hill grazings and lowland pastures. Herds of Red Deer often break the skyline on the higher ridges.

Leave the A9 road 7 kms north of Golspie and follow the minor road on the landward side (marked Doll) for 3 kms to reach a ford over the River Brora. Park beside the footbridge there (GR871045)

The Route

1. Return along the road for 500 metres to a detached house — "Tigh na Rosa". Go right, through the entrance gateway opposite (signposted "Private Road"), and follow the track west through the woods. Take the right fork, and reach open moorland over a gate (wired shut for stock) (GR867038).

2. The track swings north-west around the open hillside, passing through a second metal gate (wire fastening), and becoming distinctly heathery as it rises steadily towards the base of Duchary ridge. The ruins of a hillfort can be seen above the north-east side of the track.

3. Leave the track at its highest point and take a short detour to the hillfort's ramparts. Linger and enjoy the views north and east — as the original builders probably did over 2,000 years ago.

4. Return to the track and continue north-west, descending gradually into the head of Coire Aghaisgeig for 1 km until a burn is crossed. This section is rather soft and wet, and the old peat track is indistinct in places. Look down north-east into the wide fan at the base of the coire and you will see a considerable stone ruin which is Carrol Broch — a fine example of the type of circular defensive tower built throughout the north around the 1st century BC.

5. Follow the burn directly to the Broch and stop to explore; the entrance is well-preserved and a tree grows in the inner court. Descend a further 300 metres or so to reach the lochside track.

From there, you can follow the lochside track back to the car, or you can climb Carrol Rock (GR844078). To do so. . . .

6. Turn left and follow the track to Carrol Farm. Follow the burn up the hill, taking the right fork to the head of the coire. The ascent of the Rock (208m) over heathery slopes is straightforward from the west and offers fine views all around

7. Follow the lochside track back to the car.

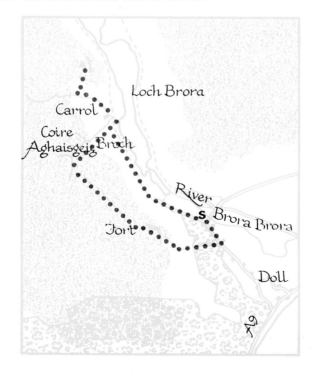

11 The Hills Of Glen Loth

Grade:	C
Distance:	7-8 kilometres — 13 kms with Ben Uarie
Footwear:	Walking boots
Terrain:	Rough path, thick heather and rolling moorland. Weatherproof clothing required. Do not attempt in poor visibility — the area has few prominent features to help navigation.
Time:	3-4 hours
Map:	OS Landranger 17

Glen Loth is the hidden way into the hills of the interior from East Sutherland. The narrow glen cuts in abruptly from the coastline and quickly disappears between steep-sided heathery hills — an easily defended place, once well-populated as demonstrated by the archaeological remains. It was also rich in wildlife of all kinds. The last wolf in Scotland is reputed to have been killed near there (in Glen Sletdale) in about 1700, an act recorded on a roadside marker stone near the mouth of the glen. Nowadays, the glen lies empty from end to end — like the wolves, Men no longer live there, and in winter months the sense of isolation becomes absolute.

Leave the A9 road at Lothbeg, 8 kms north of Brora. A single track road climbs northwards onto the hillside (sign Glen Loth), and winds its way for 15 kms over

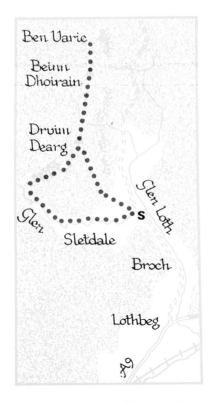

a pass at A' Chàsg and down to the River Helmsdale at Kildonan Lodge. Follow the road for 3 kms, passing the road-side ruin of Carn Bran Broch, and park near the north end of a stone road bridge at the mouth of Glen Sletdale (GR937127)

The Route

1. Cross the fence on the west side of the road and make a short climb to look at the Bronze Age standing stone, then follow a narrow path on the north side of the Sletdale Burn for 2 kms. The path is faint and overgrown in places, and there are loose sections along the steeper banks of the stream bed, where the Old Red Sandstone exposures have been weathered. Wayfinding is easy however; the open heathery slopes above the path are uncomplicated, and the line of a stock fence can be followed above the burn course for a great part of the way.

2. The burn swings north-west as the glen narrows between Càrn Garbh and Creag a' Bhodaich. Leave the burn at the south corner of Creag a' Bhodaich (GR912132), and take a line north-east, skirting the base of the stony south-east face of that hill. The line curves steeply up onto the flat saddle joining it to Druim Dearg (GR925143) (cairn) — 1.5 kms. Animal tracks can be linked to give easy walking through the thick heather

The inexperienced, or unfit should return to the car — see **4** *below. Otherwise. . . .*

3. From the broad summit of Druim Dearg, experienced hillwalkers should follow the heathery ridge northwards over the summit of Beinn Dhorain (GR925156) to Dun Uarie (628m — GR927165). This is a straightforward route, but be aware of the steep stony slopes along the east side where the hill drops into Glen Loth. (4 kms there and back).

4. From the summit of Druim Dearg, walk south down the broad, heathery ridge for 1.5 kms to reach easier ground which leads east for 1 km back to the start. The road is in view all the time during the descent, and tracks can be found for part of the way

WOLF

12 Kilphedir Broch — Strath Of Kildonan

Grade:	**B**
Distance:	**3 kilometres**
Footwear:	**Walking boots**
Terrain:	**Sheep track and heather slopes. A short walk of archaeological interest and with fine views along the Strath.**
Time:	**1.5 hours**
Map:	**OS Landranger 17**

The great inland straths of north-east Sutherland feature prominently in the prehistory and history of the North. Man has lived here for at least 6,000 years, as revealed by the abundance of archaeological remains scattered throughout the area. Life was never easy, and the early farmers always had to be prepared to defend their settlements.

The most impressive defences are the brochs, large circular stone towers up to 10 metres in height, situated on strategic hillsides or other natural features. Most are now heaps of stone, but there are a few which are still fairly well preserved and are easily accessible.

Kilphedir Broch is ruinous and appears as a great mass of grey stones tipped from a gigantic bucket down the side of the hill. However, its heather-covered defensive walls are still impressive, and it has a commanding position overlooking the River Helmsdale with fine views up and down Strath Ullie

Leave the A9 road at Helmsdale and take the single track A897 road which cuts north-west through the Strath of Kildonan and Strath Halladale to Melvich on the North Coast, skirting the Caithness border as it does so. Stop at the bridge over the Kilphedir Burn, 6.5 kms from Helmsdale, and park just off the roadside (GR989187).

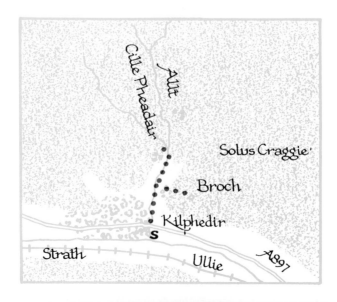

The Route

1. From the east side of the bridge, a sheep track leads uphill along the side of a stock fence, before swinging right to pass through the remains of an old crofting settlement just under the power line. The Broch (GR995189) then comes into view on the hillside above, 800 metres north-east of the roadside — an easy walk

2. Leave the broch and descend to a good path. Follow it around the side of the hill to reach a group of three hut circles on the edge of the steep side of the Kilphedir Burn; one of these has a souterrain or underground storage chamber leading out beneath its wall

3. Continue north along the steep heathery slopes to reach a further group of hut circles (GR991193) dating from the Late Bronze or Iron Age

4. Follow the east bank of the burn back to the road.

HOW A BROCH MIGHT HAVE LOOKED

13 Sutherland Gold — Suisgill Burn And Cnoc Na Beiste — Strath Of Kildonan

Grade: B/C
Distance: 8 kilometres
Footwear: Walking boots
Terrain: Stalker's path and open hillside — a good walk for fit, experienced parties.
Time: 3 hours
Map: OS Landranger 17

The Strath of Kildonan has witnessed many strange happenings in the course of its history, but few as unusual as the brief episode from 1868 to 1869 when the burn beds rang to the sound of pick and shovel and men came from far and near to seek their fortune in the Sutherland Goldfields!

Nowadays it is the world famous waters of the River Helmsdale which draw fishermen to reap a silver reward in salmon — though gold-panners can still be seen trying their luck in the great river's network of tributaries, and commercial prospecting in neighbouring hills is soon to start again. Two of the best known sites of activity were along the Kildonan and Suisgill Burns on the east side of the upper strath. Initially, cartloads of prospectors would come up from Helmsdale every day. However, camps were soon established at the burn mouth, where most of the miners lived rough, few sleeping at their claims inland among the hills, for the area around the base of Cnoc na Beiste (the hill of the beast) had an unsavoury reputation, easily scoffed at in daylight, but at dusk, a great, black, two-headed dog with glowing eyes is not to be trifled with! For the fee of £1 per month they could work their claim of 4 square metres — few fortunes were made. Licences can still be obtained from Suisgill Estate to pan the Kildonan burn, but only the stretch between Baile an Or and the old ford (GR917228) — you never know your luck — its still there waiting!

Follow the A897 road 20 kms north from Helmsdale to reach a sign post "Càrn nam Buth" (the site of the miner's camp and shop) and park at the side of the bridge across the Suisgill Burn

The Route

1. The path on the south side of the bridge starts at a well-preserved roadside Iron Age souterrain (underground store chamber), then climbs the hillside to pass under an overhead power line before dropping to ford a stream feeding the Suisgill Burn near a rough wooden vehicle bridge. The same point can be reached along the north side of the Suisgill Burn by way of well-defined path which passes a sheep fank (pen) and shed (sign "Keep To Path. No Dogs"). Beyond the bridge the stalker's path continues in towards the hills along the east side of the main stream for 2 kms past the remnants of old settlements which are dotted along the lower slopes of the bare heathery hillside — Druim nan Comhrag (the hill of the battle) — an unrecorded skirmish from the Strath's stormy past. There the stream forks, the main branch of the Suisgill Burn flows in from the east; the branch from the west is seen to skirt the edge of a large conifer plantation which fans out from the base of Kinbrace Hill. Between the two streams the track continues up the open slopes of Cnoc na Béiste (353m)

2. Follow the path across the main Suisgill Burn (GR905269), and continue north-east onto the flat summit of Cnoc na Béiste (GR912285)

3. Descend the uncomplicated slopes in a south-easterly direction, taking the best line to reach the north bank of the Suisgill Burn, and follow it back to the ford. This was a stretch of prolific activity during the height of the goldrush. As you retrace your steps to the start, bear in mind that you are probably walking over a fortune!

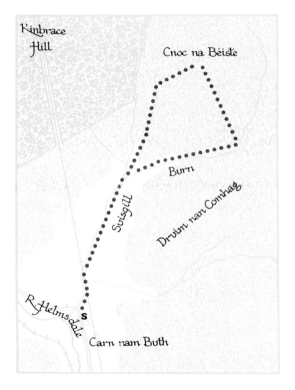

GOLD PANNING

14 The Borg To Dyke — Strath Halladale

Grade: B
Distance: 9.5 kilometres
Footwear: Walking boots
Terrain: Forestry track and rough path. A fine secluded walk with little
                climbing. A good introduction to the flora and fauna of the
                Flow Country.
Time: 3-4 hours
Map: OS Landranger 10

Strath Halladale forms the northern part of the boundary between Sutherland and Caithness. A single track road winds through it, following the line of the old drover's route which once carried herds of black cattle from the north coast glen pastures to the great markets of the south. The A897 road follows the course of the River Halladale for almost 25 kms from just beyond the isolated fishing hotel at Forsinard to its outflow into the Pentland Firth at Melvich Bay. This is the "Flow Country", a unique collection of habitats characterised by rolling moorland, unchanged since the last Ice Age; a patchwork of bog pools and dubh lochans (small black lochs) rich in plant life and home to a wide variety of the shyer rare birds and mammals. It is a spacious landscape where even the sky seems bigger; a place best savoured on foot, well away from roads and cars

The A897 road crosses the River Halladale 8 kms north of the Forsinard Hotel. Continue past the road bridge for 2 kms to The Borg (GR897511) — look for the ruined Broch on a prominent heathery knoll 100 metres east of the road — this broch gives the place its name. A vehicle track leaves the west side of the road immediately opposite, signposted "Cross Lochs Nam Breac Crocaich". Park at the junction.

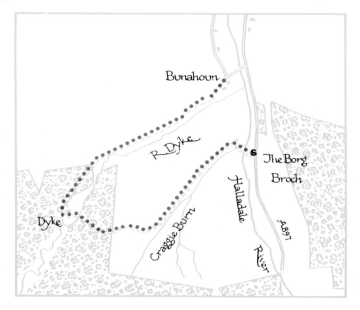

The Route

1. Follow the broad track over the River Halladale on the forestry bridge. Continue on the track up past Craggy Cottage and then south-westwards to follow the line of the Craggy Burn for 3 kms to reach an unlocked gate in the Forestry Commission fence. Look down to the north as you walk, the cluster of dubh lochans in the peatland is typical "Flow Country".

2. Inside the forest the track forks; take the north (right) branch for 1 km, crossing the bridge over the River Dyke, to reach the locked cottage of Dyke at the edge of a cleared area on the west side of the river — a delightful spot for a break.

3. Join the path at the west side of Dyke Cottage and follow it in a north-easterly direction for 1 km through the forest to reach a deer fence (GR975511) which can be crossed by a stile

4. From there, the path follows the steep, heathery banks along the north side of the River Dyke to the croft houses at Bunahoun. The course of the river is rugged in places and there are fine views north along Strath Halladale with its scattering of crofting communities on the fertile riversides.

5. From Bunahoun, continue for 200 metres to join a minor road which leads past a graveyard to cross the River Halladale, bending sharply up to meet the A897 road. Return along the road for 1.5 kms to the start at Borg.

15 Armadale Bay & Gorge

Grade: A
Distance: 3-4 kilometres
Footwear: Walking boots or wellingtons
Terrain: Heather paths and sand — wet in patches. An easy walk but be careful along the clifftop fence if children are in the party. The beach is the bonus at the finish.
Time: 2-3 hours
Map: OS Landranger 10

The Armadale Burn is a very unpretentious stretch of water. However, on its way to its mouth in the splendid horseshoe-shaped bay of golden sand which lies below the little crofting township of Armadale, it passes through a remarkably fine glacial gorge some 4 kms long.

Armadale Bay itself must have drawn the Norse longships like bees to a honeypot — its sandy beach was a perfect landing place, and the gravel terraces along its sides gave easy access inland, initially for raiding trips and then for settlement. The natives made good use of the gorge of the Armadale Burn, however, and the broch built many centuries earlier on the west side of the steep stony slopes 1.5 kms inland must have been a hard nut to crack for an attacker.

This inland route up the gorge is a fine short walk, but there are restrictions — the gorge is a Site of Special Scientific Interest and is monitored by Scottish Natural Heritage; Armadale Farm graze the surrounding hillsides and should be consulted regarding access.

The approach to the seaward side, on the other hand, is without problem; Armadale Bay and the surrounding clifftops make a delightful walk, ideal for the family.

Leave the A836 coastal road 5 kms west of Strathy, and park on the south side of the bridge at the foot of the hill on the old loop road (GR796639).

The Route

1. Walk down to cross a stile in the fence and reach the Armadale Burn; follow the west bank seawards, passing under the road bridge and on for a further 300 metres to reach a new wooden footbridge (GR795643) — this first part is muddy but it does improve. Cross the bridge and climb the heathery cliffs on the east side of Armadale Bay.

2. The cliff top is fenced, and the line can be followed northwards along the base of the Strathy peninsula for as far as desired — fine views of the rocky coastline leading out to the lighthouse at Strathy Point.

3. Once you have had enough, return to the bridge and re-cross the stile, then continue north along the west side of the Armadale Burn onto the magnificent sands below. Ghostly lights from shipwrecked seamen have sometimes been seen here in the darkness, but in the daytime it is the perfect spot to sit and unwind.

4. The Allt Beag flows into the west corner of the bay, and this too has been newly bridged, giving access to the township of Armadale perched on the cliffside above. This makes a circular walk possible, looping back eastwards past Armadale House along the A836 road. The straightforward return back along the Armadale Burn is probably preferable.

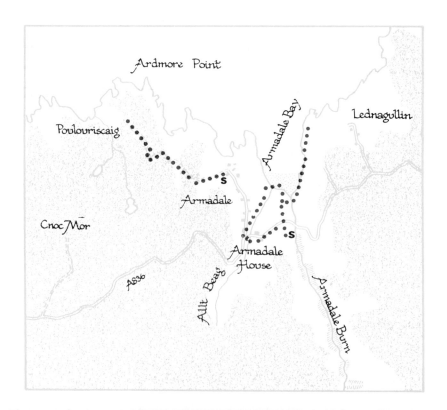

16 Poulouriscaig — The Deserted Village

Grade: A
Distance: 5 kilometres
Footwear: Walking boots
Terrain: A nostalgic walk along a good track with fine views — a good outing for a summer's evening.
Time: 2 hours
Map: OS Landranger 10

The ruined site of the deserted village of Poulouriscaig sits on the coastline of the rocky peninsula which lies between the bays of Armadale and Kirtomy. Like most of the communities along this coast, Poulouriscaig is a "Clearance Village". It was established early last century, when the people of inland Strathnaver were "cleared" from their fertile lands to make way for sheep, being forced instead to settle on the less fertile rocky coastal areas where in theory they could augment their livelihood by fishing. They had to start again from scratch, even digging out the rock and rough-hewing it to build their cottages, and wooden ploughs had to be made to turn over the soil for crops. Despite Herculean efforts, Poulouriscaig did not survive, probably because it was very small — only four families ever lived there — and it was too remote, especially in the winter months. Two of the families died out, and in the 1930's the final family moved out. On a happier note, members of the last family to leave still live in the nearby township of Armadale.

Leave the A836 road 1 km west of the River Armadale bridge and follow the narrow road on the north side for just over 1 km, to reach a junction and bus-shelter in the middle of Armadale village. Take the left (west) fork and follow it to park beside the last (white) cottage found on the west side (GR784648).

The Route

The track, which continues north from the house, leads down to a bothy above the shore — do not follow.

The track to Poulourascaig starts through a stock gate beside the house and can be clearly seen swinging westwards round the heathery hillsides beyond. After 1.5 kms, the track rises up to curve round a water tank on its south side and then continues north-west for another kilometre to reach the ruined site of the village (GR765657).

The small valley, sheltered by the hillside from south, west and east, must have seemed an attractive place to start a new life, but there is little flat land suitable for cultivation and every inch was used for survival. Both men and women worked the land and grew crops of oats, hay (for winter feed), turnips and potatoes, and they also grew common vegetables which kept them over the winter months — peat was the only fuel. There were sheep, cattle and a horse for each of the four holdings, and beef, mutton and herring were salted for use throughout the year. The younger men and women went to the herring fishing from Summer to Autumn and sent money home which had to last through the winter. It was a hard but happy way of life while it lasted, a far cry from that of the present day. The beauty and tranquillity of Poulouriscaig — the place of anchorage — is still remarked on by all who walk there to experience it.

Return by the same route.

17 Invernaver And Torrisdale Bay

Grade: B
Distance: 6-7 kilometres
Footwear: Walking boots
Terrain: Mainly sandy with peaty sections across the ridge. The start from either side can be wet for a short distance. It should be kept in mind that the sand dunes are very sensitive to disturbance, so take the greatest possible care to avoid damage to the dunes or the plants growing on them.
Time: 3 hours minimum. To enjoy the walk fully it should not be rushed — there is a great deal to see of natural, archaeological and scientific interest — a superb fine-weather walk for all the family.
Map: OS Landranger 10

The flat-topped, peat-covered ridge of Druim Chuibhe, lying between the mouths of the River Naver and the River Borgie, is a National Nature Reserve of unusual interest.

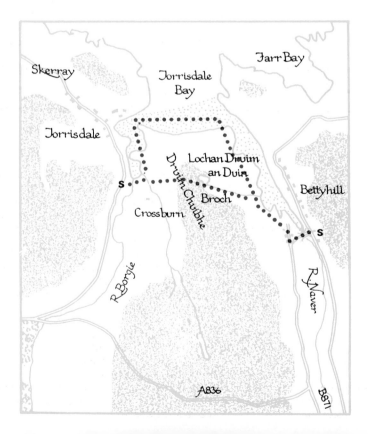

The whole Reserve covers a rectangular area, 3 kms long and 2 kms wide, rising steeply from the River Naver on the east side and falling more gently down to the River Borgie on the west. The 130 metre high ridge drops abruptly at the north end to meet the magnificent dunes and sands of Torrisdale Bay.

The bay is sheltered by rocky headlands to east and west, a natural inlet in which a sandy beach 2 kms long by .5 km broad is uncovered at low tide. The full force of the northerly gales which blast in from the Pentland Firth is responsible for the formation of the maze of shifting dunes along the foot of the northern end of Druim Chuibhe ridge, which itself is covered with blown shell and alluvial sand of varying thickness. This quirk of nature has created, within a relatively small area, "a wide variety of habitats for the finest assemblage of boreal plant communities in the north", seen at their best in the early months of the year. The area is equally rich in wildlife and in geological features.

Not surprisingly, in the early days of the Highland Clearances, its excellent grazing areas formed part of the area allocated to one of the principal incoming sheep farmers — one Patrick Sellar of Highland Clearances fame!

Two prominent flat-topped terraces flank this north section of the ridge:—
— on the Naver side, the 16m high shelf of sand and gravel has been eroded to expose a considerable cluster of prehistoric cairns, hut circles and burial cists — evidence of continual settlement along Strathnaver from earliest times. On a commanding position on the sandy buttress above can be found the ruins of an Iron Age Broch.
— on the Borgie side, the grassy lower terrace has evidence of more recent civilisation — an old fishing bothy and the local football pitch!

This northern portion of the Reserve, including Torrisdale sands, gives a splendid circular walk which can be started from either side.

From the east side, leave the A836 coastal road 1.5 kms south of Bettyhill at the foot of the hill leading inland from the village. Park at the roadside lay-by at the east side of the bridge across the mouth of the River Naver (GR710603).

The Route

1. Cross the bridge and follow the west bank of the estuary for 1 km towards the obvious raised platform which marks the settlement area. At high tide it is best to continue along the main road for a short distance to the sign "Invernaver" — from there, walk along the side road to pass the houses, cross the stock fence and continue in a straight line towards the dunes. Climb west along the path on the side of the prominent sandy gully containing a small burn, to reach the buttress above the settlements and the site of the broch (GR697610).

2. Continue rising westwards past Lochan Druim an Duin to cross the Druim Chuibhe ridge — a mere 100 metres in height at that point. From the crest of the ridge, the path (faint in places) continues to drop gently westwards to reach the broad, grassy terrace above the mouth of the River Borgie — the way ahead is always clearly in view.

3. Once down, cut northwards for 1 km to reach the Torrisdale sands, circling the dunes eastwards to regain the mouth of the River Naver.

4. Clamber over the settlement platform to explore the remains (but do not disturb anything), then retrace your outward route to the car.

From the west side To start the walk from the west side, leave the A836 road at Borgie Bridge 10 kms beyond Bettyhill, and follow a secondary road marked "Skerray" northwards for 3 kms to the mouth of the River Borgie. There is a parking place on the east side of the road (GR682612).

The Route

A path leads down to cross the river by a wooden bridge below the fishing bothy (aptly named "Crossburn"). A choice of path leads across the estuary, conveniently bridged when necessary, and a well-marked track eventually winds up onto the broad, grassy platform previously described.

Either approach is recommended.

18 | Rosal Clearance Village, Strathnaver

Grade:	**A**
Distance:	**3.5 kilometres**
Footwear:	**Sensible shoes or walking boots**
Terrain:	**Forest paths and tracks leading onto grassy grazing land which can get muddy. An interesting and straightforward family walk**
Time:	**2 hours**
Map:	**OS Landranger 10**

The Clearance Village of Rosal (Norse — Hrossa Voll or Horses Field) is situated 22 kms south of Bettyhill within the extensive forestry plantations on the east side of the River Naver. It was one of the largest of the 49 townships in Strathnaver which were "cleared" (emptied) of their inhabitants to make way for sheep farms during the infamous Clearances of the early 19th Century — an exercise by the landowners and their agents in "agricultural improvement" which resulted in the brutal depopulation of great areas of the Highlands, and which still evokes considerable bitterness to this day.

The 80 acre grassy site, surrounded by a ring dyke (wall), once supported 13 families in 18 houses and associated outbuildings. The long history of settlement is easy to see — some of the remains date back to prehistoric times.

Leave the A836 road at the junction 4 kms south of Bettyhill, and follow the B871 road along the west bank of the River Naver for 15 kms to Syre. The Naver was recorded by the early astronomer and cartographer Ptolemy in the 2nd Century AD (he called it the Naboros) and it is reputed to be a sacred river with healing powers. It is best known nowadays as one of the most prestigious salmon rivers in Scotland.

The views along the Strath in both directions are extensive, and a sense of the area's history pervades everything. Sheep and cattle still graze the hillsides but people are few on the ground. Two clues to the reason for this are passed en route.

1) A roadside stone monument at Syre marks the raising of the 93rd Highlanders in 1801 — "The Thin Red Line" of Balaclava fame. This regiment took hundreds of the young men away from the area to fight in the imperial wars of the 19th century, reflecting the value placed on Highlanders as fighting men, and their perceived expendability in every other regard.

2) The house of Patrick Sellar, the man who completed the devastation of the Strath two decades later when carrying out the orders of the Duke of Sutherland as he interpreted them, lies near Syre House.

Follow the B871 road across the river at Dalvina Bridge (signpost "Kinbrace'), then turn right (south) along the east bank of the River Naver on an unsurfaced track to reach a parking area at the forest boundary fence (GR690427).

The Route

From the carpark, the waymarked trail is easily followed through the mature pine and larch up into the "village" clearing.

The route around the open grassy clearing has interpretative boards to indicate what the site once looked like. It passes the remains of longhouses or blackhouses (the ordinary houses of the time), byres, grain drying kilns, dykes, peat beds, lazy beds (runrig cultivation strips), prehistoric hut circles, burial cairns and a souterrain (underground storeroom). To the south and west, the background of mountains is as it has always been from time immemorial.

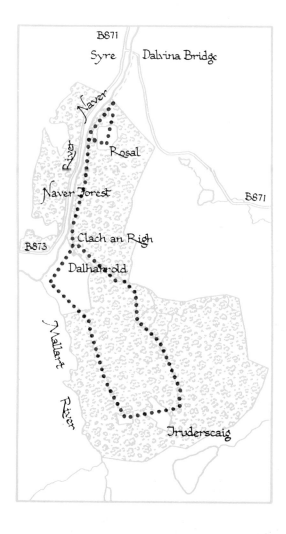

19 Clach An Righ (The Kings Stone) & Truderscaig, Rosal, Strathnaver

Grade:	C
Distance:	**Clach an Righ 7 kilometres**
	Dalharrold 8 kilometres
	Truderscaig 18 kilometres
	Complete circuit 25 kilometres.
Footwear:	**Walking boots**
Terrain:	**A mixed route depending on the distance chosen — forest track and open hillside. The two longer routes suggested are for fit, experienced walkers with proper clothing and food for a long day, who have the ability to navigate the short pathless distance between the tracks safely.**
Map:	**OS Landranger 10 and 16**

This is an extension of **Walk 18,** two forest roads to the south-east of the River Naver being linked to give a long, circular route of varied interest. Part of the route is also a waymarked mountain bike route. This walk was made possible with the help of Forest Enterprise.

The Route

1. From the parking area used for Walk 18, follow the forestry vehicle track south along the east bank of the River Naver for 3 kms to reach Clach an Righ — the King's stone — which stands on the right (west) side of the track. There is a fine example of a hut circle (remains of Late Bronze Age or Iron Age round house) just to the right of the track, which has recently been cleared of trees to protect it. This policy has been adopted for numerous other hut circles out of sight from the track. Carn an Righ is a significant Bronze Age stone circle — the largest stone measures almost 2.5 metres in height.

The track swings south-east for another .5km, then forks. Take the right hand (west) fork across the bridge to reach Dalharrold croft — the two gates are unlocked.

Like many of the inland place-names along these great northern straths, Dalharrold is of Norse origin. This is Harrold's Dale (or flat place), the site of a battle in the late 12th century in which Scottish mercenaries of William the Lion defeated the occupying Norsemen under Harold Maddadson, Earl of Orkney. Harold's own death in the battle and burial under Clach an Righ is unsubstantiated, but doubtless the bodies of his slain followers would have been disposed of locally.

2. Past the croft buildings, the track swings round open hillside for 2 kms to reach an unlocked gate in the forest boundary fence (GR683670). It then continues for another 3 kms south then east to reach a stock gate in the forest fence which encloses the site of the Truderscaig pre-clearance village. This is a protected archaeological site and bikes should be left at the gate.

The name "Truderscaig" is an interesting mixture of Gaelic and Norse, meaning "the copse (or clearing) of the wild boar" — more relevant to former times when vast areas of the original forests there were full of this animal. From the end of the track inside the fence you can decide whether to reverse your outward route to the start, or alternatively, to take the longer and tougher option and circle through the woods back to Dalharrold.....

3. Continue across the open enclosure to a stile on the forest fence and follow the pathless open forestry ride for 1.5 kms north-east around the hillside to join the end of a forestry vehicle track at the south-east corner of Cnoc Bad na Fainne (GR350349). (If in doubt, the main forest boundary fence lies to your right (south-east) throughout).

4. The vehicle track (which is not shown on the 1989 edition of OS Landranger 16), contours through the forest for 4 kms in a north-westerly direction to reach a bridge across the Allt Dalharrold (GR695377). From there, it continues for two more kilometres to the junction at Dalharrold croft.

The outward route is followed back to the carpark at Rosal.

VIKING WARRIOR

20 Crask Inn To Bealach Easach And Ben Klibreck

Grade: B/C
Distance: Crask to Bealach — 10 kilometres Footwear: Walking boots
Terrain: Easy moorland track with a short, steep, heathery section.
Time: 4 hours minimum
Map: OS Landranger 16

The A836 road south from Strathnaver to Lairg rises up over the great Central Sutherland moorland at Crask — the Gaelic name for a crossing place. This is one of the most exposed routes in the North. Empty plains roll westwards to the mountains of Assynt; to the south, the landscape is broken in places by blocks of conifers, while to the north, the wide spread of the higher mountains provide little in the way of shelter. The east side of the road is dominated by Ben Klibreck, a 961 metre (3154ft) peak whose ridge stretches for almost 10 kms to the end of Loch Naver. Further east still, the lesser hills of the Ben Armine deer forest stretch down into two great straths which open out into the Moray Firth. There are few houses anywhere.

The road reaches its highest point near the Crask Inn, 14 kms south of Altnaharra. In former years, this was a traditional stopping place for travellers going to and from sheep markets and other business in Lairg — in winter months they could be stranded there for days on end — usually without too much complaint! Park off the road.

The Route

1. Head east on the well-worn track that leaves the road a short distance south of the Inn. Follow the north bank of the upper River Tirry due east along the open flats of Srath a' Chraisg for 4 kms to reach the southern corner of the Ben Klibreck ridge. From there it swings slightly north, making a steep ascending traverse on the lower slopes of Carn an Fheidh to reach the top of Bealach Easach (360m — GR575251). This is the pass between Ben Klibreck and Creag na h'Iolaire, the first of the outliers of the Ben Armine. The view from there is breathtaking, one to be lingered over and savoured. The eye is drawn down the path ahead to the shores of Loch a' Bhealaich and onwards along the hill-flanked basin to Loch Choire. This is the very heart of two great deer forests — one of the most isolated corners in the whole of Sutherland.

The path continues to skirt the north side of the two lochs for over 10 kms to reach a shooting lodge at the north-west end of Loch Choire — no other houses are to be found.

The easy option from the Bealach Easach is to retrace the walk to the Crask bridge. On a clear day, the mountain ranges of Assynt and Wester Ross are always in view. Or.....

2. For the more ambitious walker, the open heathery slopes rising from the north side of the pass give the opportunity of a steep but straightforward ascent onto the south end of the Ben Klibreck ridge. Two circuits are possible:—

1) The shortest route is to walk on to Creag an Lochan (807m — GR576280), then west down the broad shoulder leading onto Cnoc Sgriodain (542m), from where the descent is made to the road near the cottage at Vagastie (537284) — there is a ford and a footbridge.

2) Alternatively, from Creag an Lochan, follow the main ridge northwards to climb the heather cone of the Munro top (Meall nan Con 961m), returning south to leave the ridge at its lowest point above Loch nan Uan. Descend the steep heathery slopes there to pass the south end of the loch, then follow the course of two burns and a stock fence westwards to reach the road north of Vagastie.

With both these alternatives, it is possible to meet the road further south, cutting out part of the walk along the road, but there is new forestry planting and you should pick your own route.

It must be emphasised that these longer options are for fit and experienced hill-walkers with suitable food and clothing.

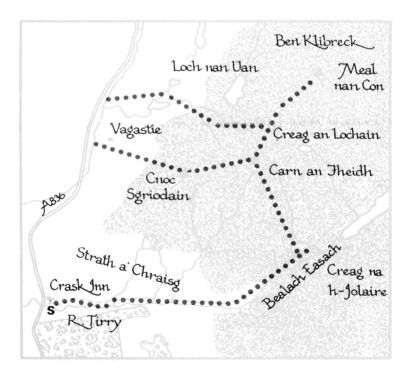

21 Dalchork Wood, Lairg

Grade: A
Distance: 6 kilometres
Footwear: Shoes or walking boots
Terrain: Easy forest track with varied natural interest.
Time: 2½ hours
Map: OS Landranger 16

This is one of several short walks into Forest Enterprise woodland, making use of the unsurfaced vehicle tracks which dissect the plantations. Cars are not allowed, but there are few other restrictions — providing one adheres to the Country Code.

The area around the community of Lairg has always been settled and is rich in archaeological and agricultural remains — burial mounds, settlements, cairns, brochs and old sheep fanks (pens). Unfortunately, many of these sites were planted with conifers some thirty years ago and are now overgrown. However, planting policy has changed, and today work is underway to clear and expose these sites within the now mature forests, and to allow visitors on foot to discover them and explore.

Dalchork Wood, to the north of Lairg, is one such area.

Follow the A836 road 1 km north of its junction with the A838, and park at the start of the forestry track on the east side of the road (GR576112).

The Route

1. Start at the gate on the east side of the road 400 metres north of the bridge, from where an unsurfaced vehicle track leads to a locked Forestry gate and stile. The clearly marked track cuts south-east into the forest for almost 2 kms, then swings north. The remains of a broch can be found on the north side of the track (GR592103), and there is a prominent circular burial mound nearby.

2. After 1 km the track veers north-west for 2 kms, past several other sites of interest, and emerges from the trees at a gate and stile. Continue for 400 metres to reach the A836 road by an unlocked gate.

3. The way south along the road skirts the rocky bed of the River Tirry, winding down into Loch Shin.

BRONZE AGE HOUSE

22 | Ord Hill Archaeology Trail & Shin Dam Forest Walk, Lairg

Grade: A
Distance: 6 kilometres
Footwear: Shoes or walking boots
Terrain: A fascinating interpretative walk for all ages. Wheelchair access for part of the Forest Walk.
Time: 2 hours plus
Map: OS Landranger 16

The Ord is a low hilly promontory on the western outskirts of the village of Lairg, overlooking the south end of Loch Shin and the fertile countryside around — it provides a unique record of human settlement in Central Sutherland over more than fifty centuries.

It is difficult for us to visualise the surrounding landscape as it would have been l0,000 years ago, and how it would have changed as the climate warmed and the plant and tree cover spread, only to be gradually removed by Man over the past 6,000 years.

The earliest remains found among the hill settlements are of the Neolithic Period — the first New Stone Age farmers who settled there some 5,000 to 6,000 years ago. Their houses are gone, but the remains of two great chambered cairn tombs on the Ord summit mark their early presence. Subsequent remains dotted around the rounded hillside form an intriguing record of Man's development right up to the present day. It is only in comparatively recent times that the community moved to its present location at Lairg nearby.

Agriculture still dominates the economy, Lairg being one of the main sheep markets in the Northern Highlands (the annual Lairg Lamb Sales are the biggest one-day lamb sales in Europe). Forestry is also important to the way of life, and it is interesting to observe that the new plantations around the base of the Ord include a significant mixture of native Scots Pine and mixed broadleaf — a turning back of the clock to the times when natural deciduous woodlands dominated.

Leave the A836 road at the south end of Lairg village and cross the River Shin by the bridge. Once across, turn sharp right (north) along the bank of the inner loch, following the signs through the Lochside houses to park at the new Ferrycroft Countryside Centre (GR578062). This is the start for both loops of the walk.

The Ferrycroft Countryside Centre uses a variety of audio visiual aids and other techniques to tell the story of the Northern Highlands from the last Ice Age to the present day. Anyone who wants to learn more about the history & archaeology of the Northern Highlands and Man's place in the environment should make a point of visiting it. It also has a Tourist Information Centre selling a wide range of literature and maps on this and other subjects.

The Route

The Ord loop of the walk encircles the hill settlement sites; the newly established Forest Walk goes north to the hydro power station dam across Loch Shin, turning back at the ruined Broch on the headland.

The Ord

1. From the left of the Centre, join the waymarked path which winds westwards up the heathery hillside to reach the television mast at the summit. On the way up you pass hut circles (all that remains of the houses is the circular bases of their walls), a "burnt mound", and field enclosures of the Bronze Age. At the summit are the neolithic chambered cairns already referred to, and just below it are a number of smaller turf covered tombs of the Bronze Age.

2. From the summit, the path swings south-east, passing near the "mystery" before swinging back along the lower hillside to the start. The "mystery", a low heather and bracken covered mound visible from the fenceline, has been compared to a small "Stonehenge without the stones" and is possibly a ceremonial site, a fortified house site..... or perhaps it started as the former and was later used for the latter!

The Forest Walk

1. Follow the track north past the Countryside Centre into the forest. Once past the pond (look out for the dragonflies and frog carvings), the trail forks. Follow the right (east) branch through broadleaf plantings to the first of two picnic sites on the lochside. Continue north along the path towards the Hydro Dam, from where it loops back south past a burial mound, broch site and hut circle. From the open ground beyond, it passes through a stand of Old Scots Pine to the fork met on the way out.

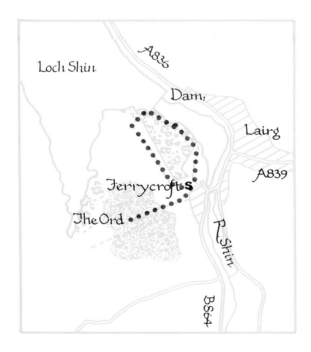

23 Shin Falls Forest Walk

Grade: A
Distance: Green Walk — about 2 kilometres.
Footwear: Shoes — wellingtons if wet
Terrain: Delightful forest paths — a "must" for children when included with a look at Shin Falls — a loop of the walk is designed for wheelchair access.
Time: 1 hour minimum
Map: OS Landranger 21

The River Shin, which flows south from Lairg for 8 kms into the Kyle of Sutherland, is of comparatively modest size for a salmon river. Its special significance for fishermen and tourists is the rocky waterslide at its midpoint — the Shin Falls. There, visitors can view at close quarters the yearly miracle of Atlantic Salmon striving to return to their birthplace to spawn. It is an awe-inspiring spectacle — the pounding they take as they avoid the temptation of fishermen's lures to launch themselves from the plunge pool into the tumbling maelstrom that they must pass to reach the gentler upper reaches of the river. The salmon can be seen leaping from July through to early Autumn.

The mainly coniferous forest along the west bank of the river give a delightful walk for all ages, the woodland plants and birdlife providing plenty of interest.

Shin Falls lies on the B864 and can be reached from Lairg to the north, or Invershin to the south — it is signposted at either end. Park at the new Falls of Shin Restaurant and Visitor Centre. This spacious new scandinavian-style timber building provides a variety of tourist services, and both walks start from the parking area. Before you start your walk look at the salmon interpretive boards, then cross the road and take the stepped pathway down to the Falls. There are railed platforms which give safe viewing and photography points — even if the salmon don't oblige, there are fine prospects along the river in both directions. Return to the Visitor Centre and you will find the signposted start of the Forest Walks west of the main entrance door.

The Route

For a short stroll follow the red marker posts; the green marked posts lead round a longer walk which loops through the mature trees.

The south section of the path runs gently down along the side of a small woodland burn to reach an open viewpoint which gives a splendid outlook across the Shin Valley to Aultnagar Lodge. The return through the wood is fraught with danger — beware of the "Forest People" and the lurking "Crocodile" — created from tree trunks by chain saw.

SALMON

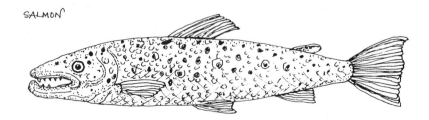

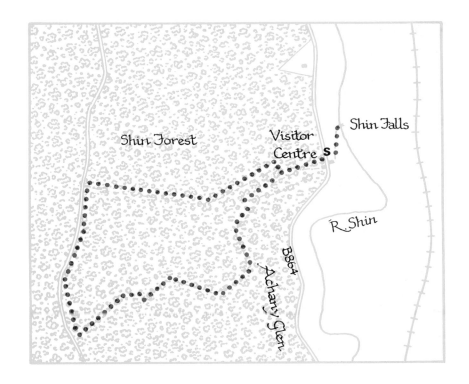

Shin Forest

Visitor Centre **S**

Shin Falls

R. Shin

B864

Achary Glen

SHIN FALLS

24 | Carbisdale Castle Forest Walk & Battlefield

Grade:	**A/B**
Distance:	**5 kilometres**
Footwear:	**Walking boots**
Terrain:	**A mixture of forest path and track with little in the way of climbing. A fine walk of varied interest for all the family.**
Time:	**2-2½ hours**
Map:	**OS Landranger 21**

Carbisdale Castle enjoys a magnificent situation on the thickly wooded west bank of the narrow neck of the Kyle of Sutherland, 5 kms north of Ardgay and close to the hamlet of Culrain. Completed just before the Great War in 1914, the site of the Castle was chosen for its proximity to the railway line north, which crosses the Kyle at Invershin. Carbisdale Castle was nicknamed "Castle Spite" — it's builder, the Dowager Duchess Blair, intended it to be a source of annoyance to her step-son, the Fourth Duke of Sutherland on his journeys to and from Dunrobin Castle by private train. This followed a spectacular family rift and court case in which the Sutherland family successfully fought off the Duchess's claim to the Sutherland inheritance following the death of her husband, the Third Duke. The building, with its palatially designed marble interior, has a most unlikely role today — that of a Youth Hostel!

This area has another claim to fame, for in 1650 this was the site of the last battle in the ill-fated final campaign of the royalist General — James Graham, Marquis of Montrose. Untypically for this expert in guerilla warfare, he was lured from his safe position on a hill onto the open ground below Culrain Farmhouse,

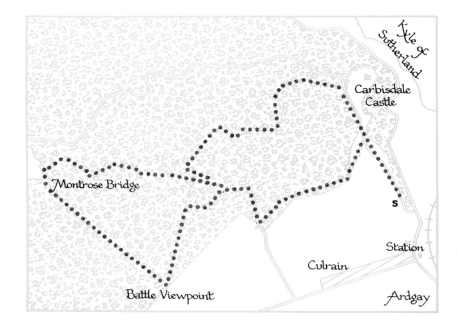

where his mainly raw and untried troops were decimated by the veteran Covenanter cavalry led by the wily Colonel Archibald Strachan. Montrose's flight north and west to Assynt and his capture there is another tale.

Drive to Ardgay on the south-west side of the Kyle of Sutherland, and from the Lady Ross Restaurant in the centre of the village, follow the single track road north-west through Gledfield to cross the bridge over the River Carron. Take the right (east) fork to Culrain and continue for a further .5 kms, to park just inside the Castle grounds (gates) — do not drive up to the Castle itself unless you are going to stay there.

The Route

1. Walk up the drive past the Castle and enter the forest (GR574955). Follow the green marker posts which lead round the shorter of the two established Forest Enterprise walks.

The path winds westwards through mature pine and Douglas Fir to reach a seat, from where it loops back to a junction. From the junction, join the longer walk by following the blue marker posts. This is the more interesting route; traversing above a delightful burn past a viewpoint seat with fine outlooks along the Achany Glen, then passing a series of waterfalls and pools that lead up to a secluded lochan with a rhododendron-covered islet (GR562952).

2. Cross the outflow at the west end of the loch on Montrose's Bridge and continue to the battlefield viewing-platform with its interpretative board explaining the layout of the battlefield of Carbisdale — a place to rest and speculate. The path then swings north to rejoin the green route, and then winds down to pass Dairy Cottage and contour the edge of the forest to rejoin the main castle drive. The open ground of the battlefield is in view on the south side.

25 | Croick Church To Oykel Bridge

Grade:	C	
Distance:	**Croick to Duag Bridge**	**12 kilometres — 5 hours**
	Croick to Oykel Bridge	**18 kilometres — 7 hours**
Footwear:	**Walking boots.**	
Terrain:	**Track/hill path. Long walk requiring transport to collect at Oykel or Duag Bridges. Take adequate clothing, provisions and map & compass.**	
Time:	**As above**	
Map:	**OS Landranger 20 & 16 (small part of)**	

Croick Church stands in a remote corner of South Sutherland at the junction of Glen Calvie and Strath Cuilleannach, 20 kms west of Ardgay. Built with Parliamentary grants by Thomas Telford in 1827 on a site provided by the local landowner, Ross of Balnagowan, the church initially had a congregation of 200, drawn from the surrounding rural communities. And then the "Clearances" reached this peaceful backwater — by May 1843 the last 18 families, 90 people in all, were to spend their final night sheltering in the walled churchyard before leaving the glen forever. Their fate is recorded in the pathetic messages scratched on the window panes of the church. Stalkers paths and sheep tracks nowadays pass the overgrown ruins on the empty hillsides — a place of great sadness.

Leave the main road at Ardgay and follow the minor road west along the River Carron. Cross the road bridge over the Carron and take the left (west) fork, signposted "Croick Church and The Craigs", following the narrow road which twists along the north bank of the river for 15 kms to the head of Strath Carron.

This is a very scenic route. Tree-lined slopes rise along the north side of the strath, and open heathery hillsides the south; birdlife is prolific and roadside deer are common; the broad, fertile floor of the strath is a pattern of well-stocked parkland, and there are frequent glimpses of the fine salmon pools and falls which make the Carron justly famous as a salmon river. Sporting Lodges abound — it is easy to see why the surrounding areas featured so prominently in the later wave of land clearances of the mid-eighteenth century.

The road junction at The Craigs boasts a telephone box. The surfaced road continues west into Strath Cuilleanach; a rough motor track cuts south to cross the Blackwater Bridge, and then skirts the edge of the Amat Forest past Amat and Glencalvie to reach Alladale — the three main sporting lodges in that corner.

Follow the motor road west for 2 kms to Croick Church and park in the small carpark (GR456914). Visit the church and wander around the tree-lined churchyard; the messages of the evicted tenants are found on the east gable windows; the remains of a broch lie outside the gate in the churchyard wall at the north-west corner.

This walk gives an inkling of the problems faced by the Cattle Drover's of long ago. It is only feasible if transport is available to collect you at the other end.

The Route

1. From Croick Church walk north-west along the track past Lubachoinnich — there are unlocked gates in places which must be refastened after use. 2.5 kms west of the house, the track leaves the floor of the strath and climbs north-west to a height of 200m to cross the broad saddle between Creag Loisgte and Cnoc nan Caorach and reach the course of a small stream — Allt nan Caisean (GR377977).

2. From there, keep to the south side of the stream initially, and make a descending traverse west for 4 kms to reach a bridge over the Corriemulzie River — Duag Bridge — near its junction with the River Einig. This was the site of a side school in former times and is long since ruined.

3. Cut back east along the south bank of the River Einig for just over 5 kms to reach a bridge (unlocked gate). The way passes through an area of ancient pinewood which is currently being cleared of introduced conifers to free up native pine and birch trees. The new fencing is to prevent deer eating the regenerating trees. From the group of houses 500 metres north-east of the bridge, the surfaced motor road swings north-west along the south side of the River Oykel for 700 metres to meet the A837 road opposite the Oykel Bridge Hotel. The walk from Duag Bridge through secluded woodland along the rocky course of the River Einig is recommended, though it is possible to drive up to Duag Bridge except in winter — if in doubt contact the stalker (Mr D Snody) at Amat (1 km south of Oykel Bridge Hotel — GR389999).

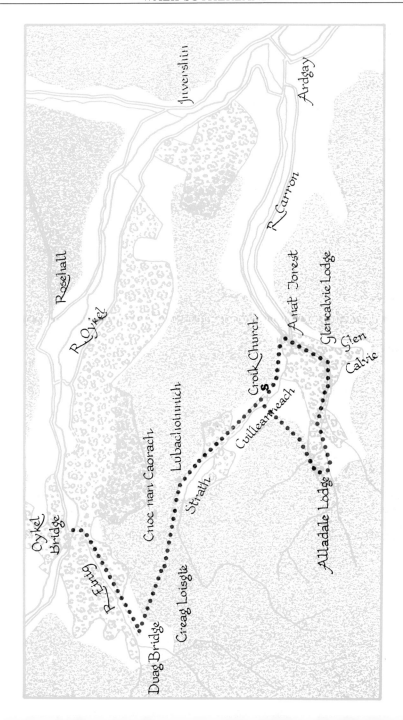

Short Alternative Up Strath Cuilleanach

Grade: A
Distance: Depends how far you wish to walk.
Footwear: Stout shoes, walking boots or wellingtons
Terrain: Rough vehicle track. A walk for all ages and abilities. You must return by the same route.
Time: Depends on distance walked.
Map: OS Landranger 20

The Route

For a gentle, undemanding route, follow the road which swings north-west along the floor of the wide valley of Strath Cuilleanach as a rough vehicle track, keeping to the east side of the winding river bed throughout. This route has no set length — the track is dry and fairly level and can be followed for many miles . . . but you must return the same way.

The atmosphere of uninhabited space is remarkable, though new tree plantations have begun to replace the once considerable sheep hirsels on the wide, heathery hillsides. There is only one solitary shepherds house to be found — at Lubachoinnich, 5 kms north-west of Croick.

Strath Cuilleanach was part of the intricate network of droving routes which led from the remote areas of the north and west to the great cattle marts of the east.

26 Croick Church To Alladale & Craigs

Grade: B/C
Distance: 10 kilometres Footwear: Walking boots
Terrain: Track, Time: 4-5 hours
Maps: OS Landranger 20

See Walk 25 for background.
For an interesting, circular, hillside route from Croick. . . .

The Route

1. Walk west from the Church for 300 metres, turn left through the gate at the far end of the roadside building, and follow the rough track down to the bridge over the River Blackwater (GR453913). Cross the deer fence on the south side of the bridge (stile), and follow the stalker's path which is clearly seen winding south-westwards up the open hillside ahead. Once over the shoulder (stile over deer fence), the path drops down to the south through woodland towards the back of Alladale Lodge.

2. Cross the burn east of the Lodge grounds and follow its course south to join a vehicle track which follows the north side of the river eastwards along the edge of the forest for almost 3 kms to a track junction (GR464891). Gates in the deer fence en route are usually unlocked. On this section of the route, groups of red deer can often be seen close to the track, grazing among the pine trees. The south branch vehicle track leads across a bridge to Glencalvie Lodge.

3. Continue along the main track for 2 kms, passing the entrance to Amat Lodge, to cross the river bridge at The Craigs. Follow the motor road west for 2 kms back to Croick Church.

27 Ravens Rock Forest Walk, Rosehall

Grade: A
Distance: 2 kilometres.
Footwear: Walking boots or stout shoes.
Terrain: Easy paths with lots of interest — trees, plants, rocks & birds. An excellent walk for children.
Time: 1 hour minimum.
Map: OS Landranger 16.

This is a short but fascinating excursion through magnificent mixed woodland in the centre of the Northern Highlands.

The woodland lies within the junction formed by the A839 road from Lairg and the A837 road from Bonar Bridge, which merge at Rosehall to head west to Assynt and NW Sutherland.

This walk, created by Forest Enterprise along the banks of the Allt Mor (Big Burn), twists through a precipitous gorge rich in tree, plant and wild life.

The starting point is reached equally well from the A839 or the A837. Leave the A839 at the bridge over the Allt Mor (GR505016), and follow the minor road (signposted "Rosehall Primary School & Altass") for 1 km to reach a Forest Enterprise signposted parking area on the right. Leave the A837 at its bridge over the Allt Mor (GR492495) and follow the minor road north for 1.5 kms to the same carpark.

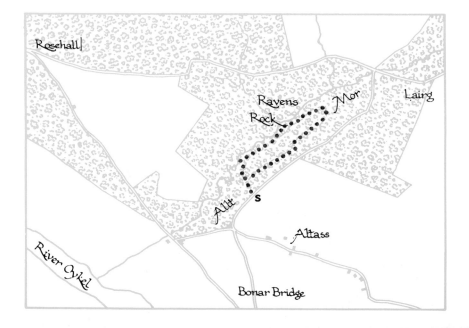

The Route

The path is well marked. Walk west down the hill for a short distance through mature woodland to reach the banks of the Allt Mor — there is a delightful picnic spot on the sheltered flat at a loop in the burn. The well-constructed path wends its way along the east bank of the stream; a spectacular route lined with beech and conifer. The final sections of this lower path pass close alongside a series of rock falls and land slips with fine views across the gorge towards Strath Oykel. From the viewpoint reached at the north end, the path swings back at a higher level, to take a gentle route through a sloping plantation of spruce and Scots pine, back to the car.

28 | Craggie To Loch Ailsh, Strath Oykell

Grade:	**B/C**
Distance:	**11 kilometres to the road-end — 15 kilometres for the complete circuit.**
Footwear:	**Walking boots**
Terrain:	**Mostly rough track giving easy but fairly demanding walking, requiring a degree of fitness. Navigation is straightforward, but the ability to read a map is advisable. Be well equipped and carry enough provisions.**
Time:	**5 hours**
Map:	**OS Landranger 15**

Strath Oykel is one of nature's great dividing lines across the mainland of Scotland. The wide valley contains the River Oykel, which rises in the tiny Dubh Loch Mor at the foot of Ben More Assynt, and embarks on a journey that takes it eastwards by way of the Kyle of Sutherland to its outlet into the North Sea at the mouth of the Dornoch Firth, a distance of almost 90 kms.

From its source in the secluded coire, fed by waters draining from the highest mountain ridges in Sutherland, its first 10 kms follow a very private course, the world of deer stalkers and hillwalkers. It flows quietly through the Benmore deer forest to Loch Ailsh, and then drops southwards, running parallel to the A837 road for another peaceful 10 kms. It enters a large, rocky gorge, and emerges dramatically through the arches of the old road bridge at Oykel Bridge Hotel. This is the real Oykel, a salmon river of the highest order, where fishermen return year after year to test their skill or try their luck. The course of the upper river gives a most satisfying walk along the forest-covered hillsides from Knock Craggie to Loch Ailsh.

Leave the A837 road 4 kms north of the road bridge at Lubcroy Lodge and park beside the small bridge at the south-east corner of Loch Craggie (GR328053). Savour the view of the unique outlines of the mountains of Assynt to the north-west.

The Route

1. Go back along the road for a short distance to reach the rough track on the left (signposted "Craggie Cottage"). Follow the track for 500metres to pass the cottage, and look down to the course of the river below. Make for the swing foot bridge at the bend in the river (GR341053) — there is no established path, but there are no problems apart from wet patches.

2. Cross the bridge and walk up a short path to reach the well-worn fisherman's track which follows the east bank of the River Oykel. Continue north-west along the track for 2 kms to reach the derelict cottage at Salachy — a delightful picnic spot on the riverbank. Two burns are crossed en route, both bridged.

3. From Sallachy, climb the west side of the burn for 500 metres up the open ride in the trees, to join a major forestry vehicle track (GR337075). This contours the wooded slopes above the river bed for 3.5 kms, emerging at the south-west corner of Loch Ailsh (GR316102). This is a truly tranquil corner — the treelined basin which holds the loch, has as a background the undulating rocky ridges of Ben More, Conival, Breabag, and all their outliers. The surrounding woodlands are rich in bird and animal life — roe deer, red deer and sika can often be seen; buzzards, kestrels, owls and curlews are regular performers. From a quiet pool at the corner of the loch, the impatient Oykel leaves its peaceful passing place through a series of rocky pools and ledges.

4. Cross the hump-backed bridge at the end of the forest track (GR312098), and go west for 3.5 kms along the rough vehicle track, to reach the A837 road at Benmore road end.

The return by the main road south-east to Loch Craggie is another 4 kms — you can arrange to be picked up, or you can enjoy the lovely views on your walk back to the starting point.

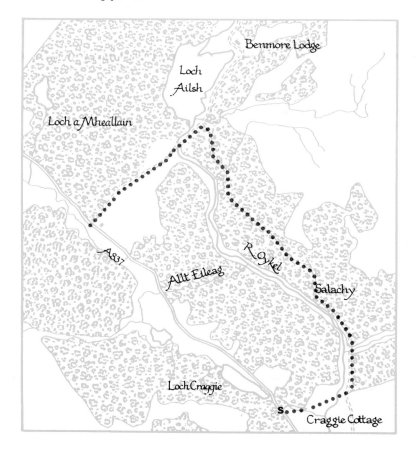

29 Borgie Forest Walk

Grade: C
Distance: **16 kilometres plus 1 kilometre for the Nature Trail.**
Footwear: **Walking boots**
Terrain: **Mostly well-marked forest track. The pathless section follows forest rides and fence-lines — take a map and compass and carry suitable outer wear.**
Time: **6 hours plus**
Map: **OS Landranger 10**

Borgie Forest stretches inland from the A836 road between Strathnaver and Tongue — the only area of mature woodland on the North Coast of Sutherland.

The forest was established after the First World War on part of the ground gifted by the Duke of Sutherland to the Board of Agriculture as part of a scheme to provide work and small-holdings for returning servicemen. Fire almost destroyed the original forest in 1942, but the surviving Scots pine and spruce are now the tallest trees in the north — giants over 30m in height. The forest habitat is further enhanced by the presence of the River Borgie and its network of tributaries. The river rises in Loch Loyal and flows through a series of three lesser lochs to reach a large waterfall about 1 km west of the edge of the forest walk; from there, its course winds through the woodland to reach the sea at Torrisdale Bay, a distance of 8 kms.

Sheltered tracks through the forest provide scenic trails for walkers and cyclists, with a wealth of natural wayside interest. Wildlife in the forest is normally shy and difficult to see, but visitors are advised not to use the tracks after dusk — unless in pairs — the mythical Beast of Borgie, a cat-headed creature with massive fangs could be encountered then — especially in winter months when hunger sets in!

Leave the A836 road 3 kms west of its junction with the B871 into Strathnaver. As the road drops down towards Borgie Bridge, a vehicle track branches south (GR680580) for 700 metres, to reach an unlocked gate in the forest boundary fence. Park there — this is the start of the walking and cycling trail.

The Route

1. Follow the track south for 6 km to the inner limits of the forest. There the track swings west, and the cycle track ends after a further kilometre. Walkers should continue west along the open forest ride for a further kilometre to reach a gate in the deer fence which marks the boundary of the planted area (GR650517).

2. Walk north down the outside of the deer fence for 2 kms to reach a sharp angle in the fenceline (GR653540). Leave the fence and make your way down the open hillside for 600 metres to reach a footbridge across the River Borgie and join a vehicle track (GR653546).

3. The track follows the edge of the river across open ground and skirts the treeline before entering the forest, emerging at the edge of a wide clearing 3.5 kms north of the bridge. Cross the clearing and pass the cottage (GR662579), to re-enter the forest on the north side. This area of woodland stretches north for 1 km, and the track emerges to rejoin the A836 road just west of Borgie Bridge.

This area contains a well-marked forest nature trail with riverside picnic tables and interpretative boards, giving a worthwhile short additional circuit.

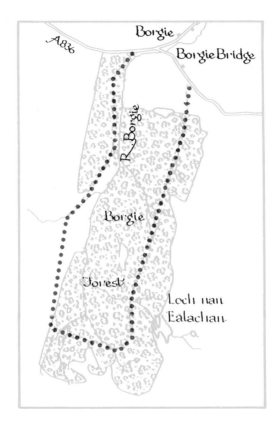

30   Caisteal Bharraich (Castle Varrich), Kyle Of Tongue

Grade: B
Distance: 3 kilometres (4 kilometres for the circuit)
Footwear: Walking boots
Terrain: Path and low hillside. Take care to choose a safe line back, well back from the cliffs.
Time: 2 hours.
Map: OS Landranger 10

The landscape around the Kyle of Tongue differs from the rest of North Coast Sutherland. The Victorian naturalist Charles St John, writing his "Tour of Sutherlandshire" in the 1840s, proclaims that, "Reaching the brow of the hill, we came into full view of the fine plantations and the bay of Tongue. The beautiful bay was as smooth as glass, the timber growing to the waters edge, and the whole scene made more striking by the abrupt and precipitous outline of the headlands both of the mainland and the islands at the mouth of the Kyle. It is worth a journey of many miles to see the Kyle of Tongue alone'' — a sentiment impossible to dispute!

A causeway carries the main A838 road across the broad, sandy Kyle. The old road can still be followed around the head of the inlet from the centre of Tongue village, and is the start of several short walks to scenic points of historical interest.

This is Clan Mackay country — the Kyle itself is ''Ceann-t-Saile a'Mhicaoidh'' — the head of Mackay's salt water, and Mackays still figure strongly in local folklore.

On a wooded promontory on the west side of Tongue village, the ruins of an important stronghold of Clan Mackay overlooks the Kyle — the object of this walk.

Park in the carpark outside the Ben Loyal Hotel in the middle of the village of Tongue.

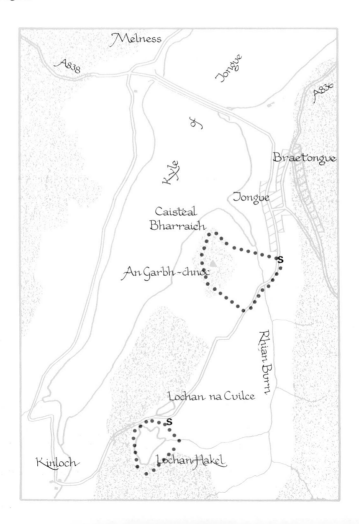

The Route

1. The path to the Castle (signposted) starts beside of the Royal Bank of Scotland opposite the carpark. Walk down the path between two walls and cross the bridge at the mouth of the Rhian Burn. The path leads down to the shore, and follows it for a short distance before climbing through the trees to reach the south side of the Castle. This is Caisteal Bharraich (Castle Varrich), a Mackay keep which is thought to have Norse origins and connections with the former Bishop of Orkney. Stop there for a while and gaze seawards across the cluster of islands, each with its story, which fill the broad mouth of the Kyle. Resist the temptation to clamber among the castle walls — these are crumbling badly and are dangerous! Either retrace your outward journey, or.....

2. Circle south with care — there are steep bluffs along the west side — and ascend An Garbh-chnoc. Swing down to the east from the heathery summit to reach a bridge on the old road to Kinloch (GR590657). Walk north along the road for 1 km to the starting point in Tongue.

31 Lochan Hakel & Prince Charlie's Gold, Kyle of Tongue

Grade:	**B**
Distance:	**3 kilometres**
Footwear:	**Walking boots or wellingtons**
Terrain:	**Rough path**
Time:	**1½ - 2 hours**
Map:	**OS Landranger 10**

Follow the road south from Tongue towards Kinloch for 5 kms to reach a pair of roadside lochs with a magnificent mountain backdrop. Open moorland stretches beyond them towards Ben Loyal — "Queen of Scottish Peaks" — a splendidly castellated ridge that rises and falls over four distinctively sculptured granite tops — seen at its very finest from this northern approach.

The loch on the south side of the road is Lochan Hakel, which figures in the story of the Jacobite Rising of 1745. In the days just prior to the Battle of Culloden, the French sloop "Hazard", laden with gold for Prince Charlie's army, was pursued around the Pentland Firth by Government ships, the chase ending with the Hazard stranded on sand bars in the Kyle. The crew and the gold were pursued by the local Militia under Captain Mackay of Melness, and were cornered beside Lochan Hakel. The story has it that the gold was thrown into the loch and that not all of it was recovered, there are still tales of cattle leaving the loch with gold pieces stuck in their hooves after they have drunk their fill!

The Route

From the roadside parking place a circuit of the loch shore gives a pleasant ramble. Needless to say, Hakel is a trout loch, and a fisherman's route can be followed all the way round.

The area at the head of the Kyle is rich in Bronze Age remains, and a particularly fine example of a Cup and Ring marked stone can be found at the south end of the loch. The views of mountain, sea and moorland are of the highest quality, and remember, if you wash your feet in the clear waters you may come out with gold between your toes — it beats gold panning!

32 Arnaboll, Loch Hope

Grade:	**B**
Distance:	**5 kilometres**
Footwear:	**Walking boots**
Terrain:	**Forestry vehicle track with wet patches and open heathery/wooded hillsides.**
Time:	**2 hours**
Map:	**OS Landranger 9**

The succession of magnificent sandy bays and sea lochs which indent the north coast of Sutherland throughout its length provide a background for some of its most spectacular scenery. Midway between Tongue and Durness the A838 road skirts the base of Ben Arnaboll (230m), to cross the narrow Arnaboll headland which juts out into the Pentland Firth and separates the two largest of these inlets — Loch Hope and Loch Eriboll. Loch Eriboll boasts the deepest natural anchorage in Britain; Loch Hope boasts the finest seatrout fishing.

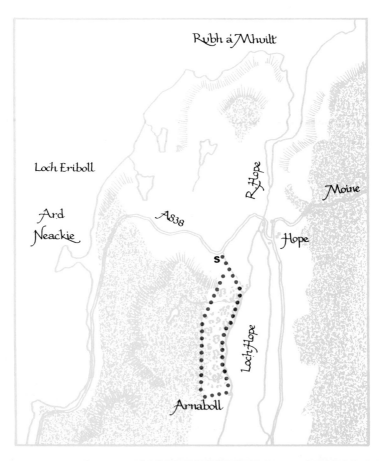

The road drops down from the empty Moine moorland to the bridge across the narrows at the north end of the Loch Hope. The River Hope enters the outer bay of Loch Eriboll, guarded at its eastern corner by the jagged headland of Whiten Head, whose 90m high white cliffs mark the end of the Moine Thrust Plane — one of the major geological earth movements which formed many of the surrounding mountains. To the native Highlander, Whiten Head was "An Ceann Geal" — the headland of the stranger — the strangers being the Norsemen who harried the coast for over four centuries.

To the south, Loch Hope stretches inland to the mouth of Strathmore, home of Rob Donn, the famous gaelic bard of the late 18th century. Nowadays, the strath has few houses — a complete generation was evicted from their homes almost two centuries ago, many being shipwrecked on their way to a new life in Canada. The shore-side farmhouse beside a little burial ground on the west side of the loch is Arnaboll — from "Arni's Boll" which means Arni's Steading — a relic name from the times of the Viking settlers. The walk in is comparatively short but the unusual views are long remembered.

Leave the A838 road where it passes over the crest of the Arnaboll ridge after climbing up from the bridge over the River Hope. Park on the south side of the road (GR467598).

The Route

1. Cross the stile on the deer-fence. Follow the vehicle track (muddy in places) down to the tree-lined lochside, and continue along it to reach open grazing land beside Arnaboll farmhouse. 1 km from the start, the track passes the tree-covered site of a Dun (northern hillfort or promontory fort) with Bronze Age cairns nearby. The cairn site at the lochside, 1 km to the south, has a diameter of 27 metres — one of the largest recorded. The view south from the track is dominated by the cliff-lined schistose terraces of Ben Hope (921m) the most northerly of the Munro summits in Britain. To the west lie the secluded giants of the Reay Estate. The obvious return route is retrace the track out. However,.......

2. Experienced walkers can cut north along the edge of the forest fence for 300 metres, then contour back through the top of the woodland to reach the deer-fence at the start. This is an exercise in careful wayfinding which need not be difficult. Be aware at all times of the rocky outcrops along the hillside, and be prepared to detour to find the easiest line. If in trouble, the descent to the track is straightforward.

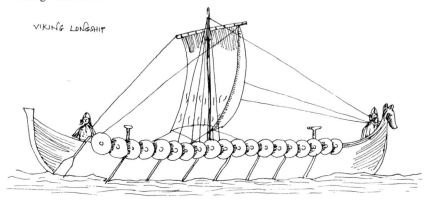

VIKING LONGSHIP

33 Loch Eriboll Wheelhouse

Grade:	B/C
Distance:	6 kilometres (8 kilometres for Portnancon)
Footwear:	Walking boots
Terrain:	Rough track and open heather-covered hillside which gives good walking. A map and compass are essential for wayfinding in the middle part — for the remainder, the road is always in view. Do not attempt in bad visibility.
Time:	2-3 hours
Map:	OS Landranger 9.

Loch Eriboll has long provided a sheltered anchorage for seafarers — Norse raiders on their way to the west, Spanish fugitives from the Armada, ships of war of more modern times, and fishermen of all nations.

The two shorelines of the 12 km long loch are in marked contrast. The east side falls steeply, straight into the sea in some parts, down to a green coastal strip in others, and there are frequent rocky outcroppings of grey, incut, Moine Schist. Heilam, where the road crossing The Moine from the Kyle of Tongue meets the lochside, was a primitive inn for the infrequent travellers in the last century; the T-shaped peninsula jutting out into the loch from the flat coastal strip is Ardneakie Tombollo — the vaulted buildings are the remains of an old limestone quarry and kilns — and make an interesting detour. The limestone was used to neutralise acid soils and is responsible for the green pastures on the narrow coastal strip along the loch.

The road from Heilam follows the shore around to the head of the loch where it passes the land-locked inlet Lochan Havurn, formed out of glacial debris.

On the west side, the road rises along the base of long, brown, heathery slopes. These stretch north-westwards on a uniformly-angled bed of quartzite to the rim of a boulder topped mountain ridge which stretches inland from Durness to Srath Dionard for almost 20 kms.

The west side of Loch Eriboll gives a fine walking expedition to reach an unusual archaeological site (wheelhouse) lying hidden from the road beyond the first skyline. The views to Ben Hope and beyond are striking.

Follow the A838 road to Laid. The road crosses a burn with houses on either side — continue north for a further 500 metres to meet a rough track which cuts south-west on the landward side of the road, immediately opposite a bungalow (GR416595). Park on the verge (off the road, not in a Passing Place).

The Route

1. Follow the track up the hillside for 500 metres until it starts to turn down towards the loch. Leave it on the bend and continue westwards across heathery slopes to reach the bank of the Allt an Lagain burn. Follow the faint pathline up the north side of the stream over a succession of quartzite ledges and water slides for 1 km, to reach a first definite junction (GR404598). There, the path fades out.

2. Continue up the right (north) branch to reach a heathery hollow with a steep rocky ridge rising along its east side. Walk carefully — groups of red deer can often be surprised as they graze. Aim for the rounded hummock ahead and scramble over the bare quartzite pavements — the site of the Iron Age "wheelhouse'' is tucked in below the crest at the north-east corner (GR405611). This circular building, dating from the 1st century AD, is remarkably well preserved — built entirely of flat quartz blocks and still roofed in places with considerable stone slabs.

A cluster of three lochans lie in the heathery basin in the hills immediately to the west. Another line of lochans can be seen along the glen opening north-eastwards, leading the eye to the sea and along the coastline. The atmosphere is difficult to describe, a place where it is easy to let the imagination turn the clock back 2,000 years.

The return walk offers three options:—

Option 1
Retrace the outward path down the burn.

Option 2
Follow the line of lochans north-east, and cut round the hillside beyond the last one (GR412615). From there, take an easy line south-east back to the track. The lochside road is always in view, the short-heathered surface gives good walking, and the views are superb.

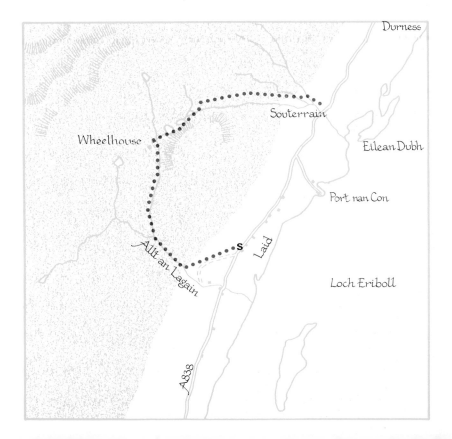

Option 3
From the last of the four lochans in Option 2, follow the outflow of the burn east to reach the A838 road just north of the little pier at Portnancon.

The hillside to the north carries an interesting relic of World War II, when Royal Navy ships and merchant convoys anchored in Loch Eriboll. Sailors on shore-leave laid out the names of their battleships in boulders on the heather. These have recently been given a facelift of whitening by the local Durness Community Council, and they stand out well from the roadside once you are aware of their existence.

Two cairns by the roadside (GR428613) mark the site of a notable Iron Age souterrain (underground food store) — wet inside, enter at your own risk.

From there, the walk back along the road to the car gives a series of fine views along the loch.

34 | Balnakiel And Faraid Head, Durness

Grade:	**A/B**
Distance:	**8 kilometres.**
Footwear:	**Walking boots, shoes or trainers.**
Terrain:	**Delightful beach and sand dunes, with a short stretch of track. A superb family walk. There is a wealth of seabird life to be observed all the way round.**
Time:	**2-3 hours or longer.**
Map:	**OS Landranger 9.**

IMPORTANT: The spectacular sand dune ridge behind the beach is very fragile — please take care not to disturb the sand wall or cause damage to the plants growing on the tops.

Durness has a unique position on the north-west tip of mainland Britain, lying as it does between the deepest and shallowest sea inlets on the North Coast! The scattered crofting townships that comprise Durness lie around the fertile area at the base of the machair covered headland of Faraid Head. Westwards, the great sandstone cliffs of Clo Mor stretch along the Parph peninsula to the true corner of mainland Britain — Cape Wrath.

The area offers many attractions to visitors. 1.5 kms east of Durness, the A838 road passes the start of a steep path leading down to Smoo Cave — a spectacular sea-cave, well worth a short detour. Inland, to the south and west, the hills offer a wide choice of expedition for all abilities. The area's famous limestone lochs need no introduction to a trout fisherman worthy of the name — and welcome also to the remotest golf course in mainland Britain! But if anything, it is for it's wealth of beautiful sandy bays and inlets covered with miles of golden beach and dune that Durness is really renowned. A walk around the Faraid headland is a rather special outing. For more information on this magnificent outpost of mainland Britain, visit the Durness Visitor Centre.

Leave the A838 road in the centre of the village and follow the single track road (signposted "Balnakeil") which climbs west for 1 km to pass the Balnakeil Craft Village, a former Ministry of Defence site converted to a Craft Village in 1964, and well worth a visit. Continue north for 500 metres to reach the carpark at

Balnakeil Church and the start of the walk. Before starting the walk, spare some time to explore the churchyard. This is the site of one of the first churches in Sutherland, the oldest part of the ruined church is Pre-Reformation (16thC AD), but the foundations are much earlier. Like all old graveyards, the stones tell some fascinating stories — a good read! Look out for the grave of Rob Donn, the Gaelic Bard, and within the church wall, the grave of Donald McMurchie, a prolific local murderer. Visit the Durness Visitor Centre for further information.

The Route

1. Cross the bridge opposite the church and walk down onto the beach in front of Balnakeil House. Built on the site of a monastery, it is typical of the style of a Highland laird's house of the mid-18th century. Go to the far end of the beach — if the tide is out you can walk along the beach at the waters edge — and join a track which leads through the sand dunes. Follow it until the dunes end (1 km), then leave it and detour north-west around the west fork (point) of the headland.

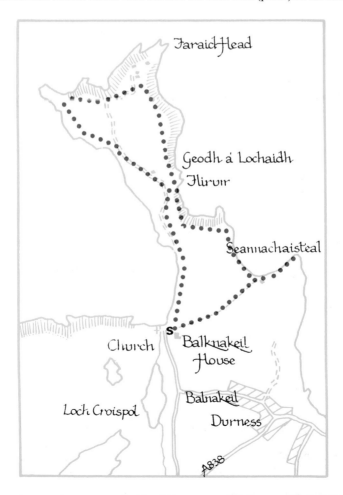

This takes you above a rocky shore line with breath-taking views westwards along a succession of delicately tinted sea-cliffs. Return east to reach the end of a fence-line that cuts off the Ministry of Defence area at the extreme north end of the Faraid peninsula.

2. Follow the line of the fence east and walk uphill to reach the cairn east of the summit of Cnoc nan Sgliat. Look eastwards along the north coast of Sutherland — Caithness and the islands of Orkney can be seen on a clear day — seascape scenery at its very best. Follow the east side of the headland back to the dunes to rejoin the outward track. Continue south along the track to reach a stone wall, then make for the east side of the peninsula, passing along the south edge of a rocky bay — Geodh a' Lochaidh Flirum — to reach an old gun emplacement on a grassy knoll. From there, follow the coastline to the south.

3.Beyond the last of the dunes at the southern corner of the bay, a track can be joined (GR403693) which takes a line west back to the start at Balnakeil. A detour left, across the north end of a stock fence, leads to the most easterly point on the peninsula — Seannachaisteal. This is the site of a promontory fort, with little to see nowadays but a rickle of overgrown stones. Its defences were formed by cutting a broad ditch across the rocky promontory and raising an earth rampart to the seaward side. Well worth a short detour for the magnificent viewpoint.

35 Cape Wrath To Sandwood Bay And Blairmore

Grade:	C
Distance:	**Cape Wrath to Blairmore — 17 kilometres**
Footwear:	**Walking boots**
Terrain:	**A walk for experienced parties — must be fit and properly equipped. This is an isolated route with no assistance readily available.**
Time:	**7 hours plus — allowing for contingencies (and not counting travel to the Cape).**
Map:	**OS Landranger 9. No dogs permitted at south end.**

Sandwood Bay is a uniquely beautiful indent in the north-west coastline of Sutherland between Cape Wrath and Loch Inchard. To reach it you have no alternative but to walk, and this has thankfully helped to limit the influx of visitors and has been a major factor in preserving its pristine condition. It is undoubtedly one of the finest wild areas in Scotland.

Sandwood Estate is now under the care of the John Muir Trust, a charity that aims to safeguard wild places while respecting the needs and aspirations of the people living and working in them.

The mouth of the Bay stretches for 2 kms — the south end is guarded by a 60m sea-washed sandstone stack — Am Buchaille — a nesting place for seabirds. From the north end, a line of magnificent seacliffs stretch towards Cape Wrath, the white lighthouse perched clearly in view. Inland, Sandwood Loch is separated from the sea by a broad bar of grass-topped dune and machair. A solitary cottage stands above the loch on the green slopes along its south-west shores — the last inhabitant tells of the peace and isolation. An eerie place at dusk, with strange sightings of a bearded sailor. Seals lie on the great, flat tide-bared rocks, and

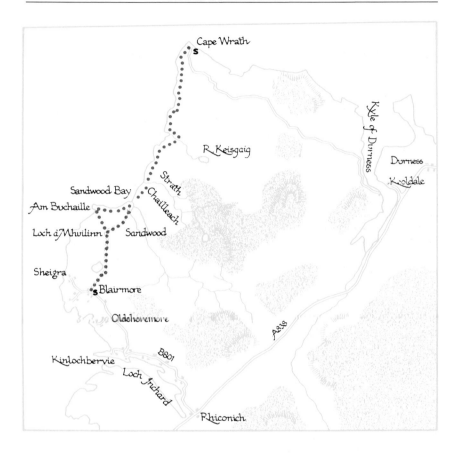

shepherds in the past have encountered green-eyed mermaids beside them. A truly magical bay.

The approach to Sandwood Bay from the north is a demanding expedition — (the easiest route is from Blairmore to the south — see next walk) — however, the walk along the north-west coastline from Cape Wrath is an unforgettable experience. The way is pathless for over 12 kms, but the underfoot conditions are good — a predominance of short, crisp heather and sandy textured clifftop. Wild rocky coastlines stretch north and south, offering up a rich variety of shades and shapes. Inland, the complete emptiness of the landscape is overwhelming.

Cape Wrath is the north-west corner of Britain — the Cape was originally "Hvarf" — Viking for turning point — and this became Parph in Gaelic, and Wrath in English. The walk starts from the lighthouse at the Cape.

Leave the A838 road 3 kms south of Durness and follow the minor road past Keoldale and the Cape Wrath Hotel to a small pier. A passenger ferry crosses the Kyle and links with a minibus service which runs across the north of the Parph peninsula to the lighthouse. The only alternative to the ferry and minibus is to walk around the head of the Kyle — not recommended!

The Route

1. Enjoy the seacliff views around the lighthouse headland, then head south along the clifftops — the choice of line is your own. There are two possible water problems en route in wet weather. The River Keisgaig, halfway along the coast, can usually be crossed at the head of the steep-sided bay at a point below the stone shelter there (GR249694). The river flowing through Strath Chailleach, 3 kms further south, can cause greater problems. The series of rocky falls encountered as the river drops to the sea can usually be negotiated with care. If these are found to be impassable, the alternative is a long detour inland to find a suitable crossing place.

2. The final approach to Sandwood is best made over the inland end of the band of finely coloured pegmatite outcrop which drops down to the river flowing out of Sandwood Loch. Cross in the rocky shallows of the outflow — the sandy section nearer the sea looks easier but it can be very soft and you can get sucked into it very quickly indeed! Follow the beach south-west.

3. You now have a choice of routes south to Blairmore, the simplest being to follow the path that leads past the string of lochs, joining a track at Loch a' Mhuilinn. The alternatives are described in the next walk.

It is advisable to tackle the walk from north to south — if you miss the last minibus from the lighthouse you are stranded for the night . . . and the Parph is the reputed haunt of the dreaded Cusaeng, Sutherland's answer to the Yeti — a creature so terrible that no one who has met it has ever survived to describe its shape (convenient for the story!) Its shadow was once seen on the hillside — it had two heads! Alternatively you must walk all the way back to Durness via the head of the Kyle — something at least one person has had to do in recent years! The key to the expedition is to have a car at the start and finish, or to have a driver to drop-off and collect.

NOTE: Much of the Cape area is Ministry of Defence property and the small island — An Garbh-eilean — is used by the RAF for live bombing practice. If you are planning this walk, check in advance to ensure that the ferry is running (is is also affected by the weather). Phone Durness (01971 511287).

CAPE WRATH

36 Blairmore To Sandwood Bay

Grade:	B/C
Distance:	From the road end at Blairmore — 16 kilometres.
Footwear:	Walking boots.
Terrain:	Track — rough and wet in patches; sandy beaches and dunes; heathery clifftop, and moorland beyond. One of the most beautiful corners of Sutherland, the sand dunes behind the bay are of considerable biological and geomorphological importance and are extremely fragile. Please leave Sandwood Bay as you find it. No Dogs.
Time:	5 hours minimum — it is difficult to leave!
Map:	OS Landranger 9

Leave the A838 road at the junction just north of the Rhiconich Hotel at the head of Loch Inchard and follow the mainly single track B801 road towards the major fishing port of Kinlochbervie. The harbour is well worth a visit, however for this walk you must leave the B801 on a minor road that cuts sharply right (north) past the Kinlochbervie Hotel and heads off towards the crofting hamlets of Oldshore and Sheigra — fine views westwards. Stop at Blairmore, 1 km north-west of the sign to Oldshore Beag. Cars should be left on the south side of the public road near the start of the signposted track to Sandwood Bay (signposted "Sandwood Bay 4 miles No Dogs"). Please take great care not to obstruct access for crofters and other people living there. Do not take your car through the gate.

The Route

1. The track leads through a gate and should be followed for 2 kms to reach the north-east corner of Loch na Gainimh. Continue for a further 1.5 kms to the south-east corner of Loch a'Mhuilinn, where the crofter's peat-track stops. This last stretch is badly eroded. Walk along the sandy shore of the loch and join a path through broken peat and sand onto a broad track leading north for 2 kms — the central cairns here are a hindrance rather than a help. Swing round the corner of Druim na Buainn — and be prepared for a view of breathtaking beauty — impossible to describe with justice. Walk down through sand dunes onto the beach.

2. Leave the south-west corner of the beach and clamber up a short, steep bank of sand and grass to the heathery hillside above. A sheep path contours west along the cliff top to reach a point overlooking the off-shore stack — Am Buchaille (GR203651). This is a coastline rich in plant life and sea birds.

From there you can return to the beach and retrace your outward journey back to the car, or . . . .

3. A short, pathless, cross country alternative route back from the stack is possible on a clear day. Follow the top of the cliffs south-east from the promontory viewpoint for 200 metres to the head of a deep-cut inlet (short fence across top). Walk inland south-east across open moorland for 500 metres, to pass between two lochans (GR205645). From there, continue up the open hillside to cross the ridge ahead at its lowest point (110m) — the outward track comes into view at the top. Descend easy heathery slopes to rejoin the outward route at the north-east corner of Loch a'Mhuilinn.

37 Around Ben Stack, Achfary

Grade:	**B/C**
Distance:	**12 kilometres.**
Footwear:	**Walking boots.**
Terrain:	**Hill track, path and surfaced road. A fine, circular walk into hidden corners with scenic views — longish but not difficult.**
Time:	**4 hours.**
Map:	**OS Landranger 9 and 15 (small part of).**

Ben Stack (721m) is the only summit of significance within the sprawling mountainous area of North-West Sutherland known as the Reay Forest to lie on the west side of the A838 road which traverses diagonally south-eastwards from Laxford Bridge to Lairg. The hill rises sheer out of the west side of Loch Stack and lies just north of the little village of Achfary. A sharply outlined conical ridge, its summit can be reached from either end with little difficulty by averagely fit hillwalkers.

This is sportsman's country par excellence. Loch Stack is one of the most renowned sea trout lochs in the country; the River Laxford, which flows north-westwards past Laxford Bridge into the tidal head of Loch Laxford, is a renowned salmon river — like most of the sealochs along the coast, the name is Norse — Lax-fjord means salmon inlet. The surrounding area formed the traditional hunting forest of the Lords of Reay, chiefs of Clan Mackay, one of the great families who ruled this part of Sutherland in the past. The forests were rich in game of all kinds — "profitable for feiding of bestial and delectable for hunting" in the words of a 17th century chronicler. The area around Ben Stack is still one of the best parts of the Westminster Estate, the present owners, and permission to walk should be sought during the main part of the stalking season — from August onwards. Incidentally, the deer of the Reay Forest were renowned for their forked tails!

Park the car at a stone building (estate stable and bothy — GR265437), 400 metres north of Loch Stack on the A838 road 5 kms south-east of the road junction at Laxford Bridge.

The Route

1. Follow the well-defined stalker's track that leads up the hill from the road. The track winds steeply to disappear round the broken heathery slopes at the north-west end of Ben Stack, and then continues for 1 km to reach a fair sized lochan — Loch na Seilge. Cross the stream which flows down into the loch. From there, the path levels and continues for 2 kms to reach a cairned junction (GR245419).

The main stalker's track (which this route does not follow), continues south-west for 7 kms through a landscape of rock, heathery hummocks, and loch-filled hollows, to emerge on the A894 road at Duartmore Bridge, 4 kms north of the Kylesku Bridge (GR198372). This is a fine cross-country expedition, but it passes through one of the main stalking areas for the Westminster and Kylestrome estates and should be avoided towards the end of August.

2. Turn south-east at the junction. The first section of the path is faint but follows a logical line on firm ground, contouring the base of heathery slopes, and soon reaching a series of marker cairns. After 1 km, the path becomes more prominent as it continues above the north bank of the Allt Achadh Faraidh River, to cross a deer fence and enter the pine forest. The views along this section are particularly fine — the rocky outline of Ben Stack dominates the north; ahead, beyond the trees, the mountains of the Reay Forest line the sides of deep passes — the old ways through the hills. Inside the forest, the way becomes a pleasant, pine needle-covered vehicle track, following the steep-sided course of the burn.

3. Leave the trees at the south-east corner of Ben Stack — the track emerges through a gate in the deer fence to join a road running past a group of estate workers houses at Achfary, joining the A838 road near an unusual black and white telephone kiosk. Follow the road north-west for 5 kms back to the start — the views to the north side are fascinating; across Loch Stack, the banded quartzite slopes of Arkle rise starkly out of the low foreground, and beyond this are seen the long ridge of Foinaven; to the left of the route, the rocky terraces of Ben Stack tower above the road.

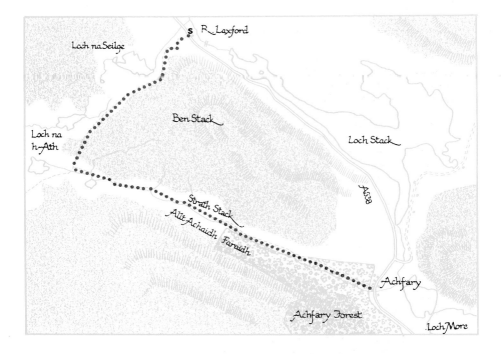

38 Loch A'Mhuillin, Duartbeag

Grade:	**A**
Distance:	**4-5 Kilometres**
Footwear:	**Walking boots or shoes**
Terrain:	**An easy walk for all abilities.**
Time:	**2-3 hours**
Map:	**OS Landranger 15**

Loch a'Mhuillin is a small National Nature Reserve lying on the west edge of a stark but enchanting peninsula, bounded by two sealochs — Loch Laxford and Loch a Chairn Bhain.

The landscape is dominated by rock and water — bare rounded humps of banded gneiss, peat bog pools, and heathery hollows filled with dark fresh-water lochans. Duartbeag is one of the few surviving deciduous woodlands, and contains the most northerly remnant of native oak in the country. The area around Loch a'Mhuillin has been deer-fenced to exclude grazing animals, including red deer, in an effort to promote natural regeneration. The reserve is rich in plant life, and the variety of habitats, including inland loch and rocky sea shore, encourages a wide variety of birds which can be readily seen. Badger, otter and roe deer live there, and the shoreline is the haunt of both grey and common seals. There is no restriction on access, but please observe the Country Code.

Leave the A894 road 6 kms south of the crofting community of Scourie. On a road bend at the foot of a hill, a stone bridge on the west side carries the old road through a rocky gorge along the north side of a stream — Allt an t'Strathain. Park beside the gate (GR179386) — cars are prohibited, pedestrian access only.

The Route

Follow the old road west for almost 1 km towards the head of a rocky cove. The road then swings north-west, to pass through a fence (gate and kissing gate). Follow the road past Loch Duartbeg for just over 1 km to a junction. The branch west leads to Duartbeag Nursery at the south-west corner of Loch a'Mhuillin. The main area of woodland regeneration lies around the north-west shores of the loch. The main through-road crosses a stone bridge at Loch a' Chreagain Daraich, and emerges to contour the low hillside for another kilometre, eventually emerging on the A894. Follow the roadside back to the start through an impressive rock cutting displaying typical colouration and veins in the Lewisian gneiss.

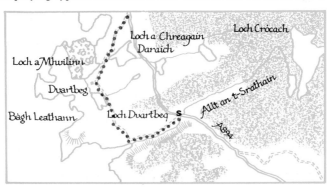

39 Kylestrome To Loch Glendhu

Grade:	**B/C**
Distance:	**14 kilometres.**
Footwear:	**Walking boots or shoes.**
Terrain:	**Good track all the way. An excellent walk for all ages and abilities. Peaceful and scenic.**
Time:	**4-5 hours**
Map:	**OS Landranger 15**

The West Coast of Sutherland is divided between the two parishes of Eddrachillis and Assynt — the boundary formed by a long twin-pronged sea loch, Loch a' Chairn Bhain, which opens westwards into Eddrachillis Bay with its host of sandy inlets and low-lying islets. Inland, the loch narrows between Kylesku and Kylestrome — it is reputed that "a strong man could hurl a stone from one side to the other"! Until recently, it required a ferry to cross the channel from Kylesku on the south side to Kylestrome on the north — this was the only link to the North Coast. Nowadays a graceful road bridge spans the gap. East of the narrows, two fingers probe inland for almost 7 kms: the north inlet is Loch Glendhu; the south is Loch Glencoul. The dividing headland — Aird da Loch — is of great interest to geologists — it is an outstanding exposure of two great earth movements — the Sole and Glencoul Thrust Planes. The head of Loch Glencoul is dominated by a prominent rocky stack — well seen from the bridge at Kylesku. This is the Stack of Glencoul, of more interest to geologists than to climbers. Beyond the small inner loch, Loch Beag, a great waterfall gushes over the lip of the Leitir Dhubh escarpment for 200 metres. This is Eas a' Chual Aluinn — the fall of the beautiful tresses — the highest in Britain. Needless to say, a beautiful maiden once flung herself from that point to escape a fate worse than death. The shores of both inlets give fine walks, the route along Loch Glendhu being less complicated.

Turn east off the A894 road at the minor junction (signposted Kylestrome), 1 km north of the Kylesku Bridge. Follow the disused ferry road for 400 metres and park at the designated area near the gateway of Kylestrome Lodge — leave the lodge gate clear.

The Route

1. Walk past the lodge and cross the stile beside a locked road gate. Continue round the wooded shore-line for 500 metres, to reach a gate in the deer fence on the north side of the road. Join the path which enters the pine trees, and follow it around the shore line for 800 metres to an exit gate at the east end of the woodland. This is a delightful section of the walk, rich in woodland flowers and scented broom, with openings through the trees giving marvellous views southwards across the inner sea loch onto the nearby cluster of islets and skerries with their basking seals. The great rocky buttresses of Quinag form an impressive backdrop.

2. Once through the deer fence, the well-maintained track winds eastwards for almost 2 kms along the base of steep heathery slopes, broken with rocky outcrops, to reach a path junction (GR247342) (cairn). The north (left) branch swings steeply up the hillside along the tumbling course of the Maldie Burn — you continue on the right track which drops down and round, to cross the burn below a fine waterfall gorge at a wooden footbridge. This is the mouth of the inner north fork of Loch a'Chairn Bhain — Loch Glendhu — the loch of the dark glen.

3. The path follows a drystone dyke for a short distance, then takes an undulating

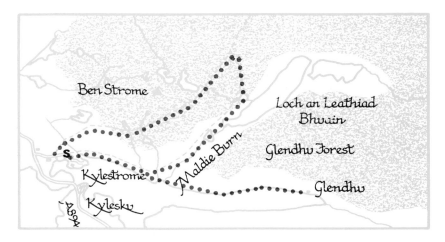

course for 4 kms, twisting round close-to and above the shoreline, with crag-lined slopes rising on the north side. Loch Glendhu Lodge can be seen throughout the walk, nestling in a grassy basin at the head of the loch; this is the obvious resting place. The lodge buildings are occupied during the stalking season, when there is a warning sign at the wooden bridge at the west side of the small burn — at other times this secluded corner enjoys a marvellous solitude.

The path continues along the shoreline past the lodge, disappearing into the narrow, rocky glen to the east, reappearing to twist up the steep headwall of the pass beyond. This is a traditional route across the mountains, pathless in part, emerging along the A838 road south of Achfary. It is still feasible but the expedition requires careful organisation.

4. The return walk along Loch Glendhu from the lodge loses nothing in the repetition — the views back are entirely different and open up many fine aspects not seen on the way out.

39b Alternative

Grade:	**B/C**
Distance:	**14 kilometres**
Footwear:	**Walking boots**
Terrain:	**Excellent stalker's path with some steep sections, but well graded. A walk to linger over and enjoy. Do not attempt if unfit for walking on long hill paths. Map and compass recommended if the summit of Ben Strome is planned.**
Time:	**4-5 hours**
Map:	**OS Landranger 15**

The north branch path passed at the Maldie Burn junction on the outward route gives a more demanding, but uncomplicated variation for fitter walkers.

1. Follow the well-marked stalker's path for almost 2 kms, making a gradual ascending traverse on the slopes above the north-west side of the Maldie Burn, to reach a wooden fisherman's bothy on the north side of a small lochan. Continue north-eastwards, up through heathery knolls and past Loch an Leathiad Bhuain, to reach a cairned junction (GR264370). There are fine views from there to the north and east across the mountains of the Reay Forest — a good spot to stop for lunch.

2. From the junction, swing back south-west: the path contours for almost 4 kms, giving a delightful walk with superb views in all directions. Steep, heathery slopes with bouldery outcrops fall to the south-east — the line of the outward path is well seen below; the north side of the path skirts a mosaic of lochans which make a foreground for the flat rocky ridge which forms the rather indefinite summit of Ben Strome (426m). A straightforward diversion from the path can be made from various points along the way for those who wish to "bag" this fairly modest top, but take care if the weather is doubtful — wayfinding can be tricky in poor visibility, even over the short distance involved. The path zig-zags steeply down to cross the outflow of the Allt Briste and skirts the corner of a rather fine lochan, richly fringed with plant life and beautifully tinted rock. Swing west from the loch and make a gradual descent for over 1.5 kms on open heathery slopes. The starting point at Kylestrome can be seen below, and the views across the sealochs to Quinag are exceptionally beautiful. Look out for deer in the sheltered hollows.

3. Pass through a derelict wire fence and drop steeply down to cross a stream bed, then walk up a few metres to reach a fence beside a roadside sheep fank (pen). Follow the tarred road for a short distance westwards, then take the path on the south side which twists down towards the treeline. A forest path leads straight along a deer fence to emerge at a metal gate near the parking place at Kylestrome Lodge.

40 — Eas A'Chual Aluinn (Waterfall) and the Marble Road From Inchnadamph

Grade:	**C**
Distance:	**24 kilometres**
Footwear:	**Walking boots**
Terrain:	**High level stalkers' tracks and paths with no locked gates. It must be emphasised that this is a long, serious walk for fit parties with hillwalking experience. Proper clothing and equipment are essential, as are sound navigational skills. Once across Bealach na h'Uidhe you are committed to a long walk out.**
Time:	**7 hours**
Map:	**OS Landranger 15**

The waterfall of Eas a'Chual Aluinn attracts numerous visitors each year. The usual start is from the west (GR241293), by a path which leaves the A894 road 5 kms north of Skiag Bridge. This skirts the south end of Loch na Gainmhich, climbs steeply up between Cnoc na Creige and Glas Bheinn, and takes a line south-east towards the top of Leitir Dhubh escarpment. This is a straightforward line, well trodden, and easily followed in clear weather.

A longer and more interesting approach is from the south — from the Inchnadamph Visitor Carpark outside the Inchnadamph Hotel at the east end of Loch Assynt.

The Route

1. Leave the Inchnadamph Visitor Carpark and walk north along the A837 road for 200 metres to cross the road bridge over the River Traligill. A vehicle track lead eastwards through a stone-pillared gateway. Follow this track along the river side past Inchnadamph Lodge, and go through an unlocked gate above the keeper's house which stands a short distance beyond. During the red deer culling seasons, a map on the gate post shows which area of the hills to avoid that day. Continue for 1 km to reach a concrete ford across the Allt Poll an Droighinn, which feeds into the River Traligill from the north-east (GR258219).

2. Leave the vehicle track on the west side of the ford, and follow the obvious stalker's path which makes a steep, ascending traverse for about 3 kms on the slopes above the north-west side of the stream. The path levels out slightly beyond a marker pole — continue for about 600 metres to reach a small ghillie's shelter and a cairned path junction (GR274240).

3. Continue on the main (left) branch of the path across the hard-surfaced shoulder of Cnoc an Droighinn northwards, to pass between two small lochans before descending a short peaty bank to wetter ground along the shore of Loch Fleodach Coire. Ford the small burns which feed into the west side of the loch (stepping stones) and continue steeply up heathery slopes to the foot of Beinn Uidhe. The cairned path there swings north-west below the grey quartzite slabs and scree slopes to reach easier ground leading onto the Bealach na h'Uidhe (GR264263). This is the pass which crosses between Beinn Uidhe and Glas Bheinn at the west end of the long summit ridge which eventually culminates on the summit of Ben More Assynt. It is the highest point of the walk (620m) and gives magnificent views in all directions.

4. The path descends a short, steep section on the north side of the ridge in a series of well-angled zig-zags before swinging eastwards below the shattered rocky walls and ledges which line the barren north slopes of Beinn Uidhe — a good area for spotting groups of red deer. The path is cairned but is slightly faint in places, and it requires concentration to follow it. If in doubt — keep low, do not climb. Swing north to cross more peaty ground and reach a well-cairned path junction beyond a narrow, heathery causeway that passes between two delightful little lochans (GR280270). An ideal picnic spot.

5. Follow the left-hand (west) branch of the path, which winds along a broad, stony shoulder for 1 km to reach a prominent burn — the feeder burn of the waterfall (GR274277). Cairns all the way.

There are now two choices of route to reach the head of the Falls. Either:—
(a) take the safest route and keep to the south side of the stream, following the cairns along heathery slopes — the path finally undulates across peat banks before dropping over a short, rocky lip, to reach the viewpoint for the Falls — this is marked by a prominent round boulder standing on the edge of the escarpment. Or **(b)** cross the burn by the stepping stones (difficult when in spate), then follow the north bank on a broad, peaty path (very dirty when wet). Cross the burn with care on large boulders before reaching the point where the water cascades over the edge of the escarpment, and follow a narrow path along the cliff top to the boulder previously mentioned. This route requires care at all times!

To view the Falls, descend from the boulder by a series of heather ledges. The drop of the Falls is better seen the lower one gets.

6. Return to the path junction and climb westwards on a well marked line which winds up through the rounded rocky terrain to reach a big cairn at its highest point (GR265281). This marks the head of the Bealach a' Bhuirich — the pass of the

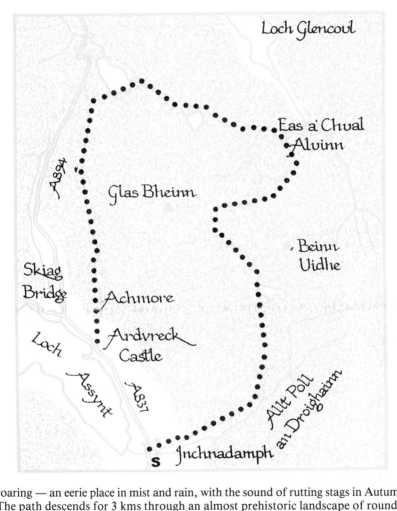

roaring — an eerie place in mist and rain, with the sound of rutting stags in Autumn. The path descends for 3 kms through an almost prehistoric landscape of rounded rocky hummocks separated by a series of dark lochans, as it makes its way towards the A894 road. The surface is stony and eroded and requires care. After 2 kms, a large cairn marks a path junction (GR251288). Loch na Gainmhich and the road are in full view.

7. Take the left-hand branch of the path which descends steep heathery slopes towards the loch side. The way along the south shore of the loch is boggy in places, improving as one rises towards the A894 road. 200 metres before reaching the A894 road, look for a broad stony cart track on the south side of the path which leads towards the base of Glas Bheinn. This can be clearly seen curving across the lower slopes of that mountain well below the prominent scree lines (GR240284).

8. You are now following the old Marble Road which was built in the late 18th century to transport marble from a quarry at Ledmore to the harbour at Kylesku — a commercial venture which did not succeed. The surface is generally good until the track drops down from the mountainside at its south end towards Achmore Farm buildings. There the line is less distinct and the path can be wet. The last kilometre is on a surfaced farm road which leads from Achmore to the A837 road. Follow the A837 road for 2 kms, to Inchnadamph along the south side of Loch Assynt.

The ruins of Ardvreck Castle and Calda House are passed en route — both have stormy histories, and friendly ghosts! Ardvreck Castle was built in 1597 by the Laird, MacLeod. In 1650, James Graham, Marquis of Montrose, was taken prisoner at Ardvreck after the Battle of Carbisdale (see Walk 24), and was taken to Edinburgh and hanged. In 1691, the Seaforth MacKenzies took possession of the castle after non-payment of a debt. The castle and lands have had several owners since. Calda House was built in 1695 by the new MacKenzie owners of Ardvreck, and it was soon at the centre of a violent dispute between this family and the Earl of Sutherland — in 1737 it burnt down in "mysterious circumstances". Some years ago, two local men were returning to Elphin with a cow when they encountered a tall grey man who emerged from the castle shadows. One man ran off, "Its a fine night" said the remaining one, and proceeded to carry on a conversation until the stranger suddenly disappeared. The stranger has often been seen since, but no-one else has ever spoken with him. The stone cairn on the heathery knoll on the west side of the road is a memorial to the two renowned Victorian geologists — Peach and Horne — who did much of their research from their base at Inchnadamph.

41 The Caves Of The Traligill Glen

Grade:	**A**
Distance:	**6-7 kilometres**
Footwear:	**Walking boots**
Terrain:	**Track and path with gentle ascents. The final stretch of track is badly eroded in places and becomes soft and dirty in wet weather. An interesting walk for all ages with plenty to see.**
Time:	**3 hours plus**
Map:	**OS Landranger 15**

The Inchnadamph Nature Reserve, which occupies the south-east corner of the parish of Assynt, contains a wide variety of habitats of exceptional natural beauty. It covers an area of over 3,000 acres of the predominantly limestone plateau south of Inchnadamph, rising from the Stronchrubie Cliffs at the south end of Loch Assynt, to the mainly quartzite lower slopes of Conival (987m) and Breabag (815m) on its eastern boundary. Two river beds form the borders along the north and south sides of the Reserve, both fascinating.

On the northern edge, the River Traligill gushes over twisted beds of limestone from the head of the glen at the base of Conival. Sometimes above ground, sometimes below, it runs a busy course through a succession of caves, pools, falls and stretches of convoluted pavement. The Norsemen aptly called this the Trollgil — the ravine of the Trolls or Giants. The more obvious of the caves are the tip of the iceberg — a vast system lies beneath the ground, with many more doubtless waiting to be discovered and explored. Above ground, the banks along the river and the hill slopes above attract numerous botanists, especially in the early months of the year. They are well-known for their rich, varied flora, some species being unique to the glen. Fenced off areas to exclude grazing and burning have been established across the reserve to research vegetation regeneration. The glen is readily accessible from the road at Inchnadamph.

Park at the Inchnadamph Visitor Carpark.

The Route
1. Leave the carpark, cross the road bridge over the River Traligill, and turn right up the track until the first ford is reached (GR251218). Cross the ford and walk up either branch of the steep stony track — they merge again at the top of the hump. Continue up the glen to the former shepherd's cottage at Glenbain. Pass through the unlocked gates some distance before and beyond the cottage — and fasten them securely after you as estate ponies graze free in certain seasons. Beyond the second gate, the track diminishes to footpath status, still easy to follow up the side of a stone walled sheep field. From the corner of the wall veer right,

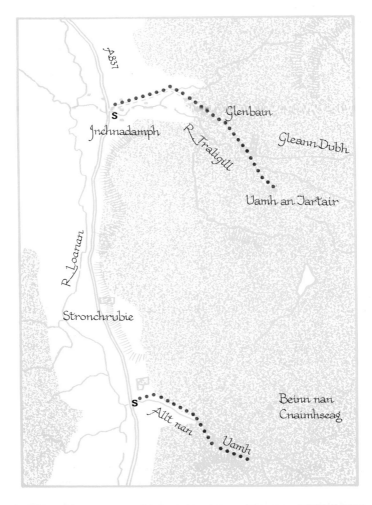

to skirt a wooden hay shed, and continue below a small conifer plantation to reach the River Traligill at the mouth of Gleann Dubh (GR271211). The left (north) branch of the path continues along Gleann Dubh on the north side of the River Traligill to the base of Conival — a hillwalker's route onto the Munro tops of the Ben More Assynt ridge.

2. Follow the right (south) branch of the path which crosses the stream by a small wooden footbridge beyond the signpost, then a broad peaty track through the heather leads up to the three obvious cave entrances at the head of the glen (GR275206). The last one reached has a domed entrance to a sizeable inner chamber — this is Uamh an Tartair — the place of the roaring — an obvious stopping place with fine views westwards down the glen along Loch Assynt, with the shapely ridge of Quinag towering along its north shore. To the immediate north of the cave entrance, steep slopes sweep down from the quartzite capped summit ridges of Conival and Beinn an Fhurain into Gleann Dubh.

3. Return to the footbridge over the River Traligill and turn left (south) along the bank of the stream to a waterfall pool and cave entrance (GR271209) — there, the now dry bed of the river bends north-west, down through the glen to Loch Assynt; the water slides down under the cave mouth and disappears, to follow an underground course. Follow the bed of the river for 700 metres on the north sides unusually shaped continuous pavements of weathered limestone, the steep rocky south bank is rich in plant life and the bed contains pools of surface water, rich in colour. Leave the burn bed opposite a large waterfall and walk up the slope north, to reach the wooden shed passed on the outward journey (GR267214).

Return to Inchnadamph down the track.

42 Allt Nan Uamh Bone Caves

Grade:	**A/B**
Distance:	**4 kilometres**
Footwear:	**Walking boots**
Terrain:	**A mixture of well-graded paths with some short sections of traversing above steeply angled, gravelly hillside which require great care. A good walk for all ages unless nervous of heights.**
Time:	**2-3 hours**
Map:	**OS Landranger 15**

The Allt nan Uamh (burn of the caves), which forms the south boundary of the Inchnadamph Reserve, is similar in nature to the River Traligill. This is a lovely corner of Sutherland, still unspoiled once you get past the fish farm hatchery. The sides of the glen throughout its length are rich in plant life associated with the underlying limestone. The Bone Caves are easily located on the prominent limestone crag which stands 1.5 kms east of the start, above the south side of the bed of the stream. These are among the most interesting palaeontological and archaeological sites in Scotland. Excavations have produced the bones of animals of the last Ice Age and suggestions of habitation by Upper Palaeolithic Man — it is still easy to imagine those Stone Age dwellers looking down on a hostile landscape from this natural refuge in the cliffs.

Beyond the caves, broad heathery slopes lead up onto the ridges of Breabag — the grey-domed, boulder-covered summit is the eastern boundary of Assynt, often covered with a mantle of rolling cloud. It was a mountain which gave problems to the early surveyors of the area in the 1780's, who declared "the air is so thin and cold that there is no hope of approaching the summit except in summer — and also — well dosed with copious draughts of warming spirit". Despite that, it is found to be an attractive mountain with a relatively easy way up onto the ridge giving superb views of Ben More Assynt and the head waters of Glen Oykel.

The walk starts at the fishfarm 4 kms south of Inchnadamph on the A837. Go through the roadside gate on the north side of the road beside the Allt nan Uamh (GR153179), and park beside the fish farm.

The Route

1. Follow the track past the fish hatchery tanks on the north side of the stream. The path, which rises eastwards along the hillside into the glen, has been upgraded by Scottish Natural Heritage. It climbs through thick bracken above the north side of the stream to pass a rather splendid little waterfall and pool, then continues along the floor of the glen for 1 km to the point where the true source of the stream is found to bubble up from the foot of a limestone outcrop in the hillside, just below the pathline — Fuaran Allt nan Uamh. From there on, the main bed of the stream is normally dry, apart from the accumulation of surface drainage water during bad weather.

2. Continue eastwards along the glen for 600 metres to reach a cairned path junction and an inscribed boulder. The main track continues eastwards along the north side; the south branch crosses the boulder-filled bed of the stream. The prominent limestone crag which rises on the south side of the glen ahead displays several distinctive cave entrances at the top of a steep glacis slope. The newly constructed path on the south side of the Allt nan Uamh is easily followed — a series of stone steps zig-zag up from the crossing before contouring eastwards along the heathery slope to the west end of the crag, from where it traverses above a short exposure of crumbled limestone before taking a steeper angle up to the entrances of the caves. Be careful on this section — the path is narrow.

The outlook from the cave mouths is remarkable, one that never seems to pall. The ledges above the entrance domes are covered in a profusion of plants; the heathery, red-tinted slopes of Beinn nan Cnaimhseag on the opposite side of the glen are the preserve of herds of red deer — sometimes difficult to pick out and always aware of your presence. Birds of prey soar above the cliff tops.

3. A series of paths cross the face of the slope below the cave mouths leading to the east end of the crag. This is the line of the return route. The paths are narrow, the slope below is steep, and there are several large limestone boulders at the base. At two points on the way across, the path line crosses a short runnel of small, loose, limestone scree — extreme care should be exercised and younger members of the group should be kept under control. The path angles down gently from a point below a prominent rocky niche at the east corner of the crag, to reach the mouth of a shallow heathery gully. Turn down towards the bed of the Allt nan Uamh, and cross over to the north side to join the return path to the road. Take care crossing the bed of the stream, wet boulders there can be treacherous.

43 | Gleann Leireag From Loch Assynt

Grade: B
Distance: 6.5 kilometres
Footwear: Walking boots
Terrain: A mixture of wet and dry hill-paths. A straightforward, scenic walk requiring no great effort.
Time: 3 hours
Map: OS Landranger 15

The uninhabited area of moor, loch and mountain lying between Loch Assynt and the south shore of Eddrachillis Bay displays a fine example of typical West Sutherland scenery — a magnificent mountain ridge of finely terraced sandstone capped with pale quartzite, rearing up from a rolling plateau of peat and heather-covered gneiss, scoured into a maze of water filled hollows. Hard to live in, but beautiful to behold! The walk across its centre is both straightforward and beautiful.

The path starts from beside the cottage of Tumore (GR184267) on the A837, just over 5 kms west of the junction with the A834 at Skiag Bridge. A sign on the north side of the road just beyond the cottage marks the start of the public pathway to Nedd on the north Assynt coastal road.

The Route
1. A well marked path passes behind the house and climbs steeply round the hillside for 1.5 kms to reach a gate in a stock fence at the top of the Bealach Leireag — the broad saddle — which straddles the glen between Creag na h'Iolaire and the cliff lined ramparts of Quinag.

2. From there, the path drops continuously in a north-westerly direction to reach the B869 minor road — a large stone cairn lying back from the east side of the verge marks the exit point at the top of the brae, 1 km east of Glenleireag, at the head of Loch Nedd.

The path deteriorates in quality as you progress westwards — the way is distinctly wet in patches, and there are sections where the line of the path is faint (this section is earmarked for improvement). Wayfinding, however, is easy — the line of the path keeps to the north side of Uidh an Leothaidh, the stream flowing into Loch an Leothaid; it rises to contour the north side of that loch, and then bends round its smaller neighbour, Loch Uidh na h'Iarna, to join the outflow of the Abhainn Gleann Leireag. Before the stream bed drops down into woodland, the path swings north round open hummocks to reach the B869 road.

Unless a return walk is visualised, arrange to be met by transport at the north end.

The walk is dominated throughout by the great sandstone ramparts which form the west side of Quinag, the last distinctive "mountain" in the chain of Torridonian sandstone which stretches the length of the western sea board from Applecross to Cape Wrath. The line of cliffs stretch for almost 3 kms from the saddle, across the ridge at the south end — Bealach a'Chornaidh, to the craggy, rounded terminal buttress of Sail Gorm (776m), the second highest of the three summits. This is one of the finest views of the mountain. In contrast, the views to the north-west and south are dominated by water — lochs and seascapes abound.

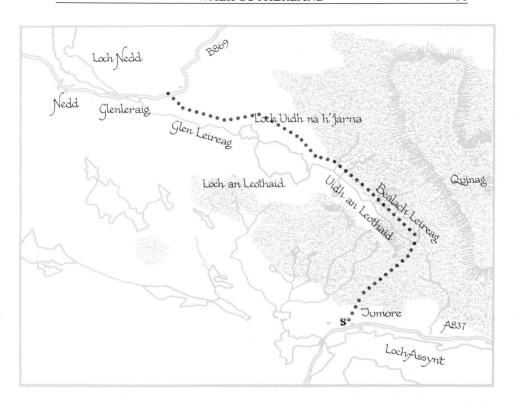

QUINAG

44 Clachtoll From Achmelvich

Grade:	**B/C**
Distance:	**5-10 kilometres**
Footwear:	**Walking boots**
Terrain:	**A mixture of sand dune, hill path and heathery sea cliff offering superb seascapes. Map essential for north section — pathless, some wayfinding necessary. The road is never far from your route, so if in difficulty — turn inland! Suitable for all ages as far as the old mill (2) — the last section north is not for young children.**
Time:	**3-4 hours minimum**
Map:	**OS Landranger 15**

The coastline between Lochinver and the headland of Stoer is one of the most beautiful stretches on the west coast of Sutherland — a succession of magnificently sculptured cliffs and headlands, indented throughout with secret rocky inlets and beautiful sandy bays. It is a classic example of a West Coast crofting area — a populated seaboard where the crofters have limited coastal grazing for sheep and cattle, and access to the sea. Inland, the harsh but beautiful landscape is of little use agriculturally — it is more a place for visiting sportsmen and tourists. Life is hard here and crofting is still the mainstay — but these are not dying communities, the area having recently gone through a period of re-birth. In 1992 the innovative Assynt Crofter's Trust was able to purchase the land on behalf of local crofters from the liquidators handling the affairs of the previous landowner — a Swedish property company. Ownership of the land they croft has breathed new life into the community, and many exciting projects are being planned.

The main attraction of the area is its scenery, wildlife, activities like fishing and walking, its culture, and the all-pervading sense of peace and tranquillity. The beach and bays around Achmelvich give pleasure to hundreds of visitors each year. Some come to relax along the marvellous sandy coves, others to enjoy the rich natural history of the area. Further north, Clachtoll has its own contributions; the fine remains of a defensive broch on the shoreline at the north end of the bay, and to the south, the remarkable split rock of Clachtoll — A'Clach Tuill — a great slab of detached rock. This is the debris of a fallen sea-arch, which crashed into the sea 150 years ago, the event being foretold 200 years earlier by Kenneth Mackenzie — Coinneach Odhar Fiosaiche — The Brahan Seer. He foretold that the "Clach Tholl near Store will fall with a crash so loud as to cause the Laird of Leadmore's cattle, to break their tethers" — the prediction was fulfilled in 1841 — the laird of Ledmore's cattle strayed 20 miles from home to within a few hundred yards of the arch and bolted when it fell into the sea! He was eventually burned for his powers of second sight — something he presumably failed to predict.

Leave the A837 .5 km north of Lochinver, and follow the scenic B869 coastal road which circles back round the north of Assynt by way of Stoer and Drumbeg, to rejoin the A837 south of Kylesku Bridge. The single track road twists through a woodland-dotted landscape of rocks and lochans for 2 kms, to reach a minor junction beyond a road bridge (sign Achmelvich). It follows a picturesque route around the north shore of Loch Roe for another 3 kms to reach the beach carpark at Achmelvich. The walk starts from there.

A nature trail hugs the coast from Achmelvich Bay to the sandy inlet of Port

Alltan na Bradhan — the Countryside Ranger at Achmelvich Beach Hut should be contacted at the start for further information on this route.

The Route

1. Go through the croft gate and follow the track north for 400 metres to reach a small lochan. Bear left and follow a well defined winding footpath around and over a series of heathery hillocks for fully 1.5 kms. This is the old route from Achmelvich to Alltanabradhan. The old path swings inland to the north-east for almost 1 km, then angles sharply north-west, rising to contour a rounded heathery hump and join a newly constructed motor track which services a cluster of new houses above the head of a sheltered bay (GR058259), part of the Cathair Dubh Estate chalet development. Access inland from the B869 coastal road is for walkers only.

2. Follow the northerly branch of the new road. The Right of Way continues past the ruined cottage of Alltan na Bradhan on the north side of the developed area, and the well defined path crosses a broken stone dyke there. Climb down the steep-sided defile, passing through a fence to reach the bed of a stream coming in from the north-west. This is the site of an old meal mill used by the surrounding communities — the old mills stones and mill race are still there. Walk down towards the sandy beach of Port Altan na Bradhan and cut north-west across the flats at its head (GR052263).

3. Sheep tracks can be followed up round the rough shoulder on the north side

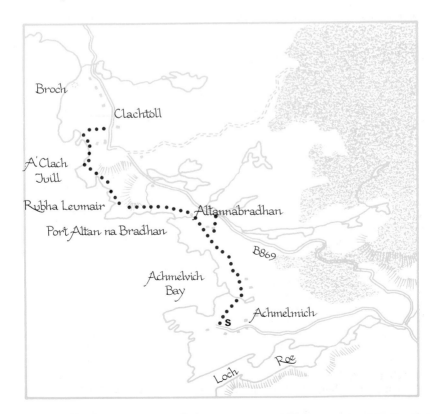

of the bay, dropping west to cross a burn flowing down through a small open glen. Take a line up the broad heathery slope on the west side, and follow a series of cairned heathery tops across the base of the rocky shored promontory of Rubha Leumair — a picturesque Gaelic name to conjure with, it means "the headland of the leaping whale"! Across the bay, a small flat-topped headland juts out to the west, with a distinctively coloured, small, sandy inlet tucked into the corner at its base — your next target.

4. Descend inland and follow a faint path-line across the bare, rounded headland, which falls in towards the sea at its eastern edge. This is the only tricky part of the route — the slabs are easy-angled and offer a good line, but be careful if wet.

5. Once over, cross the old stock fence and walk out onto the flat, grassy top of the headland to see the Split Rock of Clach Toll. Contour the headland and return to the fenceline, go through the wooden gate beside a ruined house and make a way inland to the road.

6. Head south along the road. The view westwards is limited, but the view inland is one of constant change as the road switchbacks through crags and past a succession of plant-ringed lochans.

7. Leave the road at the Cathair Dubh signpost opposite Loch an Ordain (GR058260), then swing south to rejoin the track back to Achmelvich. Do not loiter near the junction — the black dog of Creag an Ordan roams the lochside hollows — a two-headed beast belching fire, with horns, a human face, and eyes like glowing peats — even if you don't see it, you may hear its peals of laughter as it spies on you.

45   Stoer Head And The Old Man

Grade:	**A**
Distance:	**7 kilometres**
Footwear:	**Walking boots**
Terrain:	**Sheep tracks and heathery hillside. A straightforward walk for all ages — sea-cliff scenery at its best.**
Time:	**2-3 hours**
Map:	**OS Landranger 15**

The Stoer Peninsula juts out into the Minch from the Sutherland coastline between Eddrachillis Bay and Enard Bay. A lighthouse stands on a grassy platform above a prominent cliff of sloping sandstone at the south corner; the rocky promontory which forms the tip of its northern corner is the Point of Stoer — the most westerly feature of the Assynt mainland. The first of the Norsemen who sailed there named the headland "Staurr", meaning "a pole" — they were obviously describing the 70m high sandstone stack which stands off-shore, 800 metres south-west of the Point — this is the "Old Man of Stoer", a wave-lapped playground for seabirds and climbers. The headland carries a scattering of crofting communities and local sheep graze freely along the clifftops, oblivious of the danger; the rocky coastline is a nesting area for a wealth of birdlife.

The walk starts from the Stoer Lighthouse (GR003330). From the south, follow the B869 scenic coastal road to a road junction at Stoer Village Hall. The scenery en route shows marked contrast: seaward, turquoise waves break along the jagged shoreline; landward, you look across a distinctive landscape of rounded rock and loch-filled hollows. Take the west fork and climb past the isolated lochside schoolhouse for just over 2 kms to a cross-roads (GR042318). Turn west and follow the single track road for almost 4 kms around the open headland to reach the lighthouse at the south-west corner of the peninsula. As you drive, the hills of Assynt and of Coigach sprout up along the horizon — a magnificent skyline of isolated peaks and ridges. It is easy to believe that the Norse gods practised there before they created their own mountains back in Norway.

Park below the lighthouse.

The Route

1. Follow the sheep tracks north along the coastline. Stop for a moment at the partially-detached sandstone flake on the cliff edge 100 metres from the start — look west for a splendid view of the lighthouse on its spectacular perch. 1 km from the start, the path crosses a shallow gully (GR008336) — the south side is badly eroded and can be awkward on the way down, the grassy north side is easier. Continue for 1 km to look down across a rocky inlet — the Old Man of Stoer

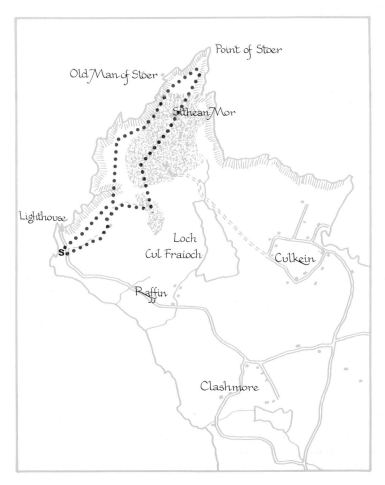

is in view ahead. From there, the way rises north-west along the lower slopes of Sithean Mor — the big fairy hill — and then drops down the steep heathery slope at the north-west end of that hill, to reach a flat open terrace overlooking the sea stack.

2. Continue north-west towards the Point of Stoer. The tip of the headland is fenced to stop sheep, but is easily reached and worth the visit.

3. Turn south and skirt the clifftop — the view along the coastline to the north is very rewarding. After 500 metres, turn inland and climb the easy slopes to the cairn on Sithean Mor. Head towards the radio mast which stands on the low hilltop to the south — the line of a path can be followed for most of the way, dropping down to pass a small lochan before rising up to the mast. From there a track winds back to the start.

46 Culag Wood, Lochinver

Grade:	**A**
Distance:	**2-3 kilometres**
Footwear:	**Shoes or walking boots**
Terrain:	**Graded, marked path — excellent family walk.**
Time:	**1-2 hours depending on route taken.**
Map:	**OS Landranger 15 and special Trail Leaflet.**

The Culag Wood covers an area of low hill ground lying between the south end of the village of Lochinver and the crofting community of Strathan. The east side of the wood is bounded by sheltered waters of Loch Culag; the west side by the sea. The original organised planting was done in 1847 by the 2nd Duke of Sutherland, an event inevitably recorded on a carved rock close to the start of the new nature trail. Spruce, larch, beech and sycamore were introduced to augment what remained of the original species. The area is now a community woodland which is being managed by an energetic group of local people and organisations for the benefit of the community, and for the interest and pleasure of visitors to the area. It is planned that future management of the woodland should generate employment locally, both through various types of timber operation, and through tourist-related activities. The nature trail, which has been created through the woodland, is the result of the efforts of a group of local naturalists and enthusiasts with assistance from various outside bodies. A trail leaflet and other specialist information is available from the Assynt Visitor Centre & Tourist Information Centre. Development of walks within the woodland is an ongoing process.

Park in the harbour carpark just beyond the Culag Hotel.

The Route

1. Walk back past the hotel and turn right along the road leading between the playing field and the Lochinver Fish Selling Company. Continue due south through the industrial area, and pass the large fuel tanks. Follow the rocky track which ascends the hill (signposted) — the nature trail starts at the top of this. A large water storage tank is passed as you enter the wood — from there on, follow the numbered posts which correspond to the printed trail guide.

The line of the made path crosses the wood from north to south to reach a marked junction (GR090217). Turn right (west) there, and pass a ruined croft house to descend through mixed woodland to the White Shore. The path seen to swing to the north is closed at the time of writing — it is to be included in future developments of the trail.

2. Enjoy the view north across the mouth of Loch Inver, and explore the beach before climbing back to the path junction. A section of board-walk leads east for a short distance to reach another junction. The north branch twists up to the open viewpoint (seat) with some unusual views of the surrounding mountains. The main track continues south-east to emerge on the road to Inverkirkaig beside an old crofthouse (GR094215).

3. Follow the road back north along the shore of Loch Culag for almost 1 km. Turn left at the bridge over the Culag River and return to the carpark.

47 | Inverkirkaig Falls And The Fionn Loch

Grade:	**B**
Distance:	**8-9 kilometres**
Footwear:	**Walking boots**
Terrain:	**A well-trodden footpath, steep and stony in places, with wet patches near the head of the Falls and at the final section before Loch Fionn. A good family walk — allow plenty of time. Children must be kept under strict control at the Falls viewing point.**
Time:	**2-2½ hours**
Map:	**OS Landranger 15**

The Assynt area of Sutherland has been described as "a maze of lochs set around by mountains", and this is no exaggeration. Isolated mountains like Suilven, Canisp, Quinag, and Stac Pollaidh rear up like dinosaurs out of a low rocky plateau of hard Precambrian gniess. This in turn is pock-marked by myriads of lochs and lochans, some landlocked, others feeding into notable river systems.

One of the most serpentine of these river systems starts from Cam Loch, a catchment for various lochs and streams in the east of the area. This loch twists south-east into Loch Veyatie, which then runs north-west, eventually narrowing to become a winding river flowing into the Fionn Loch. In reality, the three lochs are almost one. Below the Fionn Loch, the river emerges as the River Kirkaig, a much more lively water which leaps over a sheer 20m fall to enter a rocky ravine, emerging after 4 kms into the sea at Kirkaig Bay. This 17 kms line of loch and river, which forms the district boundary between Sutherland and Ross-shire, passes through some of the finest mountain scenery in Scotland.

Drive along the unclassified road from Lochinver to Inverkirkaig, which leaves the south end of the village at the road junction beside the old bridge east of the new Culag pier. The road climbs south between the school loch (Loch Culag) and Culag Wood, following a mad, circuitous route along the rocky coastline to bend into Ross-shire over the road bridge on the Kirkaig River, 5 kms south of Lochinver. Park in the carpark at the bridge (GR086193) below Achins Bookshop and Tearoom.

The Route

1. A signposted path starts opposite the riverside carpark. Go through the kissing-gate and walk up the short stretch of tarred road to join the path that leads through the trees along the north side of the River Kirkaig — be sure to close the two metal gates passed on the way down to the edge of the river. The path passes several salmon pools along this low-level stretch of the river — look out for fish moving through, especially if the water-level is high.

2. 2 kms from the start of the walk, the path climbs steeply away from the bed of the gorge and takes a much higher line along the open, heathery slopes which line its upper sides. This path gives spectacular views down the rocky course of the Kirkaig, and to the mountains of Coigach to the west. After 1 km, the path reaches its highest point, and the rounded dome of Caisteal Liath on Suilven comes progressively into sight to the east. 400 metres on, a junction in the path is reached (marked); take the broad peaty track on the south side and follow it down towards the Fall — the first part has become eroded, however the final descent to the viewing places is on rocky steps. The view points give good views, but be careful, the drops into the fall poor are sheer.

3. Return to the junction and continue along the main path for just over 1 km to emerge at the west end of Fionn Loch. This final section of the path, which circuits the heathery headland at the outflow of the river, can become rather wet and boggy, but is well worth the inconvenience — the view from there is dominated by the classic angle of Suilven — the entire length of its triple-peaked sandstone ridge is in view. Everything else is secondary.

Retrace the outward route back to the start.

Climbing Suilven — From the river outflow, the path swings round the end of the loch and follows the north shoreline for almost 5 kms. The route onto Suilven lies north-east — a rough walk of 1.5 kms leads across to the base of the route up onto the Bealach Mor at the centre of the ridge. This is a longer and more serious exercise, requiring proper equipment and hillwalking expertise.

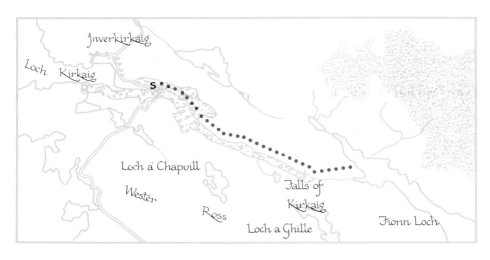

48 | Glen Canisp To Elphin

Grade: C
Distance: 19 kilometres
Footwear: Walking boots
Terrain: A mixture of track and hill path, with one short, wet, lochside section. A long route for fit walkers with proper equipment.
Time: 7 hours plus
Map: OS Landranger 15

This is one of the classic "big walks" across the Northern Highlands. The route follows an obvious line from Lochinver to the crofting township of Elphin on the south side of Assynt, following a continuous succession of lochs and streams between two of the most notable mountains in this remarkable area — Suilven and Canisp. It is a journey through a fisherman's paradise — the way passes more than 30 lochs of varying character and size in the course of a mere 20 or so kilometres. Few of these are regularly fished. Loch Druim Suardalain, which laps the front of Glencanisp Lodge, is a dream of a loch, with trout, sea-trout, and even a possible salmon as the prize; the Cam Loch at the south-east end of the walk, is considered to be a wild brown trout loch with few equals in an area. For the remainder, their contents remain a mystery — one which is perhaps best left unsolved — stories abound of creatures rising on these lonely waters to confront solitary fishermen close to their boats. Long-necked creatures, with no ears and heads like red deer hinds with great saucer eyes — they would gaze for only a second or two then swirl back below the surface — undoubtedly they were Each Uisge — the water horse. The fishermen were all sober-living, truthful men, of high repute.

The walk can be made from either end equally well, it is here described starting from the north. A good single track estate road heads east to Glencanisp Lodge from the south end of Lochinver village. Follow the track for 1.5 kms to reach a parking area overlooking the west end of Loch Druim Suardalain. This gives the first of the many fine views of Suilven — Caisteal Liath (731m), the highest of the three tops, is seen as the Norsemen saw it from their longships — The Grey Pillar — its rounded dome towering up out of a sea of rocky hillocks. Cars must be parked there, the road to Glencanisp Lodge is private, pedestrian traffic only. It should also be noted that mountain bikes are discouraged because of damage to the estate-maintained paths.

The Route

1. Walk down the road for 800 metres to cross a cattle grid at the entrance gate beside Loch Druim Suardalain. Follow the road which branches behind the lodge and go through a gate. A broad track continues for 3 kms to reach a cairned junction with a path coming in on the north side beside a walled enclosure. Suileag, an open mountain bothy, is reached 400 metres north-east of the path junction. (The north path winds across country to reach the A837 road at Little Assynt — 5 kms — a walk for another time).

2. Continue along the north side of the Amhainn na Clach Airigh for 3 kms to the bridge at the north-west end of Loch na Gainimh (GR169194). A cairn on the south side marks the turn-off for Suilven, and as an added aid to navigation, the name of the mountain has been traced in small stones on the heather verge!

If tempted to add the ascent of Suilven to the walk, remember that it adds considerably to an already lengthy undertaking — something for experienced and fit hillwalkers only.

3. The main track continues for 3 kms south-east, along the north side of the loch. 500 metres east of the bridge mentioned above, a cairned path junction is reached (GR174193). The left (north) branch rises steeply up the west ridge of Canisp, disappearing high on the red-tinged slopes above. The lower, main branch continues along the loch side to meander through a narrow steep-sided defile which opens out at the west end of Loch Fada (the long loch). Look upwards as you pass through there, the heads of inquisitive red deer hinds are normally seen peering down from the heathery shelves above.

4. Another path junction is reached just above the corner of the loch (GR198174); follow the south (right) branch which drops down across the shallow outflow of the burn. Climb up round a short steep corner and continue to rise gently along the south side of Loch Fada. This is a bare, open stony ridge, which gives easy walking — the way is clearly cairned for 2.5 kms. The path drops down from the east end of Loch Fada and bends sharply south (large cairn); it then rises steeply up a broken, peaty slope onto the crest of a broad, flat ridge leading towards the north shore of the Cam Loch. The route is still cairned and as you move south and the heather underfoot gives way to stone. At the south end of the ridge, the path swings south-eastwards down sloping pavements of white quartzite (slippery when wet) to reach the loch-side (GR220137).

5. The path line fades somewhat across the slightly marshy mouth of the burn (narrow crossing, open to variation), then follows the north shore of the loch, climbing in places over heathery banks to reach a kissing gate in the deer fence. Follow the path until the sandy shore line of a small bay (horseshoe bay) is reached at the east corner of Cam Loch. Leave the lochside at the inflow of a small burn, and follow the path eastwards towards the lowest point in the ridge ahead; from there the road comes into view. Continue round a grassy corner for 200 metres and join the A837 road from Ledmore Junction to Elphin (wooden gate in stock fence and parking area) (GR229121).

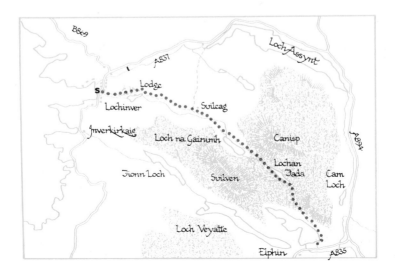

49 Uamh An Tartair (Cave), Knockan

Grade:	**B**
Distance:	**4 kilometres**
Footwear:	**Walking boots**
Terrain:	**Mostly along old peat road with a short distance on heathery hillside. Minimal navigation but take a map. A good family walk — remember to keep children under control on the rim of the sinkhole.**
Time:	**1½-2 hours**
Map:	**OS Landranger 15**

The crofting townships of Knockan and Elphin which lie scattered along the south-east boundary of the Inverpolly Nature Reserve, make a fine walking base for this corner of North West Sutherland. The magnificent mountains of Assynt and Coigach curve round them to the north; the hinterland of the Cromalt Hills to the south is a rolling landscape of hill, moor and peat — magically empty except for sheep and deer. The area lies at the edge of the Moine Thrust Plane, the meeting place of two contrasting rock types — moine schist and limestone. It is seamed with burns and caves, its surface dotted with lines of emerald green sinkholes, marking the course of hidden waterways through the underlying limestone beds. Many of these underground systems have now been explored and are well recorded. However, the majority can be only be entered by properly trained and equipped cavers. Fortunately, a few of the more spectacular features can be seen by ordinary walkers. One of the best known caves is Uamh an Tartair — the cavern of the great noise — a huge limestone arch through which the water of the upper Knockan River (Abhainn a'Chnocain) slides dramatically underground, to disappear from the floor of a 30 metre deep chasm. A birch tree on its rim is the only sign of its presence. The site is easily reached from the road through Knockan, and gives a fairly short and very pleasant walk.

Drive to Knockan, 5 kms west of Ledmore Junction. An unclassified loop road leaves the south side of the main road 300 metres west of the bridge over the Knockan River. Follow the loop for 150 metres to cross a cattle grid — a wooden gate can be seen on the east side between two cottages (GR214105). Park off the road there (do not block the road or access).

The Route

1. Follow the peat track which leads out onto the open moorland, taking care to fasten the gate. It should be noted that this is sheep country with stock in-bye at most times of the year — dogs should be left in the car, especially during lambing. Walk along the peat track for over 1 km to reach a junction beside a limestone outcrop (GR218100). Take the west (right) fork of the track and continue for just over .5 km to the point where the track bends down steeply east towards a ford in the stream below.

2. Leave the track and follow the heathery shoulder on the west side which rises above the bouldery course of the Abhainn a'Chnocain onto a rounded top. The prominent rock-fall below the west side of the heathery crag is normally dry — the river beyond has begun its underground course. Skirt the rim of a huge bracken-lined depression which lies below the north side of the small rounded top of the shoulder. Once through the heathery gap, the course of the Abhainn a'Chnocain

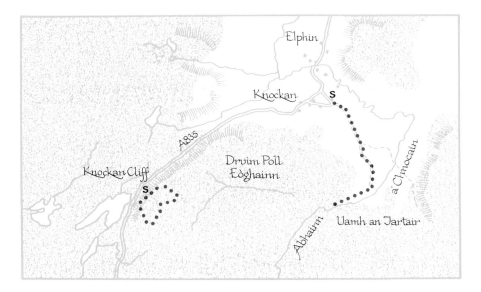

can be seen coming down from the wide upper valley beyond. Look down the heathery slope immediately ahead and you will see the tree marking the top of the sinkhole. Approach with caution — it is a long way down from the lip of the hole!

Explore the surrounding rock features, the limestone pavements are rich in plant life and assume weird shapes, and the diverted course of the main stream is equally intriguing. Retrace the outward route — wayfinding is tricky and diversions are discouraged — many parts of the surrounding hillsides have been designated Sites of Special Scientific Interest.

50 Knockan Cliff & Nature/Geology Trails

Grade:	**B**
Distance:	**1.5 kilometres**
Footwear:	**Walking boots**
Terrain:	**Marked nature trail with some steep sections — miss out the clifftop walk if nervous of heights.**
Time:	**1 hour plus depending on your interests.**
Map:	**OS Landranger 15**

Knockan Cliff straddles the boundary between Sutherland and Ross-shire — to the north and east is Assynt in Sutherland; to the south and west, Coigach in Ross & Cromarty. The cliff rises from the highest point of the A835 road which winds across the south-west corner of Assynt from Ledmore Junction to Ullapool, skirting the Inverpolly National Nature Reserve. This is Scotland's second largest reserve. Scottish Natural Heritage own the small Knockan area around the cliff itself, the remainder being managed in an agreement with three private estates — Inverpolly, Drumrunie and Eisg-Brachaidh. Conservation and regeneration of the native vegetation, with all its associated wildlife, is the main work on the reserve.

The cliff itself is one of the main features of the geological interpretative trail. It illustrates the sequence of rock exposures which makes this area internationally important — generations of students have come there to complete field work studies. The main area of the reserve, spread out along the north-west side of the road, comprises five well-known mountains. In the Inverpolly Forest lie Stac Polly, Cul Beag and Cul Mor; to the north, in the Glencanisp Forest, lie Canisp and Suilven — the whole providing ". . . a framework of peaks that together make a mountain landscape unique in the whole of the Scottish scene".

Leave the A835 road 3 kms south-west of the crofting communities of Elphin and Knockan — a sign on the north side of the road indicates the Knockan Cliff Nature Trail and Information Centre on the south side.

The walk starts from the parking area. To make the most of the numbered Geological/Nature Trails, obtain the explanatory leaflets from the information hut and then walk north (left) from the indicator pillar at the base of the cliff.

GOLDEN EAGLE